ANCIENT GIANTS

"*Ancient Giants* is a well-researched blend of myth, legend, academic literature, newspaper accounts, and oral traditions attesting to the reality of giants in our past. The ubiquitous nature of giant lore is stunning in its own right, and the author takes us to every corner of the globe to display that this mystery is more than mere fiction. The fascination with giants exists to this very day and is firmly rooted in the collective unconscious, most likely because it is a historical reality. A very worthwhile addition to the ancient mysteries genre."

Jim Vieira, coauthor of *Giants on Record* and star of History Channel's *Search for the Lost Giants*

"Legends of giants permeate all cultures and eras. Isn't it time we reviewed the evidence with open minds? Xaviant Haze does just that in *Ancient Giants*."

Andrew Gough, historical mysteries documentary presenter and researcher

"*Ancient Giants* is a whistle-stop tour of giant mythology and discoveries from around the globe. If you have ever wondered why giants seem to be a universal theme in mythology and religious lore, Xaviant provides a one-stop shop of the bizarre and spectacular world of oversize people."

Bruce Fenton, author of *The Forgotten Exodus: The Into Africa Theory of Human Evolution*

ANCIENT GIANTS

HISTORY, MYTH, AND SCIENTIFIC EVIDENCE FROM AROUND THE WORLD

XAVIANT HAZE

Bear & Company
Rochester, Vermont

Bear & Company
One Park Street
Rochester, Vermont 05767
www.BearandCompanyBooks.com

Text stock is SFI certified

Bear & Company is a division of Inner Traditions International

Library of Congress Cataloging-in-Publication Data

Names: Haze, Xaviant, author.
Title: Ancient giants : history, myth, and scientific evidence from around the world / Xaviant Haze.
Description: Rochester, Vermont : Bear & Company, [2018] | Includes bibliographical references and index.
Identifiers: LCCN 2017049030 (print) | LCCN 2017049233 (e-book) | ISBN 9781591432937 (pbk.) | ISBN 9781591432944 (e-book)
Subjects: LCSH: Antiquities—Miscellanea. | Giants—History. | Excavations (Archaeology) | Human remains (Archaeology) | Paleoanthropology Miscellanea.
Classification: LCC CC175 .H39 2018 (print) | LCC CC175 (e-book) | DDC 930.1—dc23
LC record available at https://lccn.loc.gov/2017049030

Printed and bound in the United States by Lake Book Manufacturing, Inc.
The text stock is SFI certified. The Sustainable Forestry Initiative® program promotes sustainable forest management.

10 9 8 7 6 5 4 3 2 1

Text design and layout by Debbie Glogover
This book was typeset in Garamond Premier Pro with Adobe Jenson Pro, Gill Sans MT Pro, Hypatia Sans Pro, and Trajan Sans Pro used as display typefaces

To send correspondence to the author of this book, mail a first-class letter to the author c/o Inner Traditions • Bear & Company, One Park Street, Rochester, VT 05767, and we will forward the communication, or contact the author directly at **www.xaviantvision.com**.

Contents

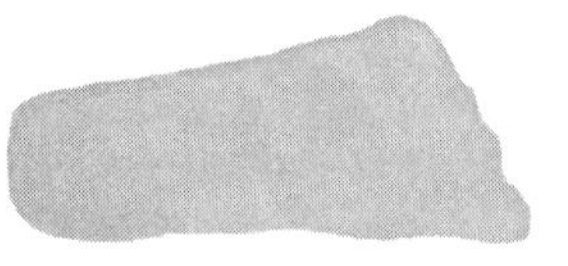

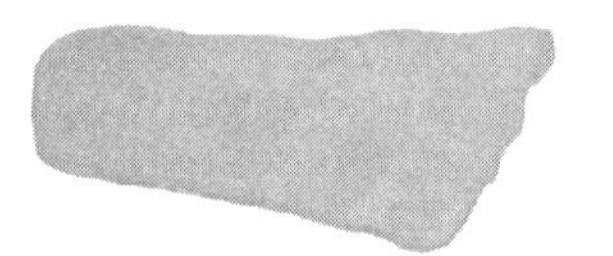

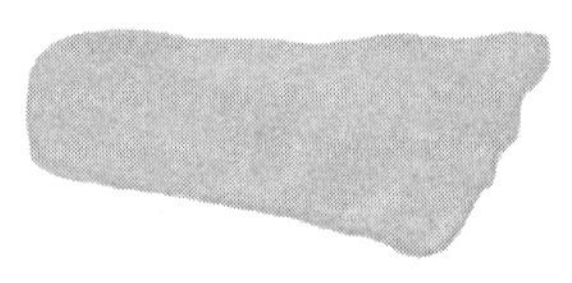

INTRODUCTION

Antediluvian Structures

The most effective way to destroy people is to deny and obliterate their own understanding of their history.

George Orwell

Of all the ancient mysteries handed down by our ancestors, the megalithic monuments remain the most puzzling, especially given that their exact dates and methods of construction remain unknown. Also unknown are the actual builders of these immensely spectacular stone structures. Mainstream academia pretty much glosses over these megaliths that can be found all over the world, assigning their creation to the will of the people or slaves being forced to haul gargantuan stones, weighing tons upon tons. Lost or buried in the mainstream arguments explaining these megaliths are the native or local histories that attribute their construction to a race of giants from a forgotten era.

The folklore of ancient Europe is full of tales starring giants who build massive stone monoliths and battle their way toward the Irish shores. The mysterious lands of Russia have also been slowly revealing their hidden ancient giant history with newly discovered megalithic structures being unearthed at a quickening pace. It seems there

Fig. I.1. *Stonehenge*, John Constable (watercolor, 1835)

is a direct mythological connection between ancient giants and the prehistoric megalithic monuments that stand thousands of years later as immense rock icons of a lost civilization.

From the Holy Lands and across the oceans to the lands of the Native Americans, all of humankind's earliest written and oral accounts speak of an advanced race of beings, commonly referred to as "giants." These giants were supposedly a hybrid species fathered by a sophisticated culture that ruled Earth before the last great flood, as much as 11,500 years ago. In fact, modern science is pointing out daily that humans are a hybrid species by admitting that recent DNA tests on the Neanderthals and the newly discovered Denisovans indicate that they share genomes that come from a completely unknown, unidentifiable group of people.[1] DNA from one Neanderthal discovered in a Siberian cave in 2013 suggests an interbreeding of multiple ancient humanlike groups in Europe and Asia more than thirty thousand years ago.[2] These results also include an unknown human ancestor and paint a world full of varying characters similar to those found in Tolkien's *Lord of the Rings* universe. Could the genomes from the forgotten race of ancient giants provide the mysterious missing link those DNA hunters are looking for?

Mainstream academia teaches that giants, cyclops, and other cryptozoological beings are nothing more than myths, and the bones that ancient humans believed to be giant bones were misconstrued, being nothing more than prehistoric animal bones. That is the official (and end of) story for the establishment when the topic of ancient giants is discussed. But there is much more to this story, perhaps a bit too much more than many in high academic positions are prepared to admit (especially when doing so could jeopardize their livelihoods).

Genesis 6:4 says:

> There were giants in the earth in those days; and also after that, when the sons of God came in unto the daughters of men, and they bare children to them, the same became mighty men which were of old, men of renown.[3]

In Hebrew versions of this passage the word *Nephilim* is used instead of *giants;* this controversial word is derived from the Hebrew verb *nafol,* and means "to fall," implying that the Nephilim are the fallen race of giants who ruled the world before being destroyed by God in a global deluge that submerged the antediluvian realm.

The Roman Jewish historian Flavius Josephus wrote about megalithic pillars (the great pyramids of Giza?) that were constructed before the flood by a race of giants who feared a global deluge. It was the hope that the monuments would survive to inspire future generations of humans. It turned out that not only did some of the monuments survive but so, too, did the giants. In *The Antiquities of the Jews* Flavius Josephus writes:

> These kings had laid waste all Syria, and overthrown the offspring of the giants. . . . There were still then left the race of giants, who had bodies so large, and countenances so entirely different from

Fig. I.2. *Pyramids at Giza, Egypt,* Louis Haghe.
Wellcome Library, London, Wellcome Images.
(colored lithograph, 1848)

> other men, that they were surprising to the sight, and terrible to the hearing. The bones of these men are still shown to this very day, unlike to any credible relations of other men.[4]

Although now relegated to children's bedtime stories, the tale of David versus Goliath was once seen as more than a morality fable. It was an accepted part of history.

Flavius Josephus continues the history lesson of David, the new king of ancient Israel, and his fight to remove the once mighty race of giants along with the Philistines from the Holy Lands.

> A little afterward the king made war against the Philistines; and when he had joined battle with them, and put them to flight, he was left alone, as he was in pursuit of them; and when he was quite tired down, he was seen by one of the enemy; his name was Achmon, the son of Araph, he was one of the sons of the giants. He had a spear, the handle of which weighed three hundred shekels, and a breast-

Fig. I.3. *David and Goliath,* Rembrandt
(etching on paper, 1655)

plate of chain-work, and a sword. He turned back, and ran violently to slay their enemy's king, for he was quite tired out with labor; but Abishai, Joab's brother, appeared on the sudden, and protected the king with his shield, as he lay down, and slew the enemy. . . .

> When the king heard that the Philistines were gathered together at the city Gazara, he sent an army against them, when Sibbechai the Hittite, one of David's most courageous men, behaved himself so as to deserve great commendation, for he slew many of those that bragged they were the posterity of the giants, and vaunted themselves highly on that account, and thereby was the occasion of victory to the Hebrews. They had a man who was six cubits tall, and had on each of his feet and hands one more toe and finger than men naturally have. Now the person who was sent against them by David out of his army was Jonathan, the son of Shimea, who fought this man in a single combat, and slew him; and as he was the person who gave the turn to the battle, he gained the greatest reputation for courage therein. This man also vaunted himself to be of the sons of the giants. But after this fight the Philistines made war no more against the Israelites.[5]

Clearly, some of the descendants of the Nephilim survived to be talked about in later mythologies before being slowly erased from history. However, since their mysterious first appearance in times immemorial, giants have morphed into a Jungian archetype, capturing the imagination and becoming part of the collective subconscious. From Paul Bunyan to Jack and the Bean Stalk, giants have remained a huge presence in the cornerstone of myths, legends, and traditions from around the world.

Irish mythology, for example, is full of exciting giant tales, one of which is the legend of the giant seafaring Fomorians and their leader, Balor, who led them to the Irish shores after surviving the Great Flood. Nobody knows where Balor and his Fomorians came from, but some scholars suggest that these pre-Celtic giants might have been from Atlantis. The ancient British lands of England, Scotland, and Wales contain many megalith monuments that legend claims were built by surviving Atlanteans. Ancient Britain was even called Albion in honor of one of the giant kings of Atlantis. It's possible that Atlantis was even part of the Irish isle at one point in prehistory. Some scholars believe that Irish Atlantis was submerged by the flooding caused by a rogue comet, which triggered a shift in the earth's crust. This dramatic Earth event instantly shrank most of the existing landmasses of ancient Europe and created chains of rocky islands along its outer wake. The Atlantean giants that survived the cataclysm could be responsible for the megalithic structures of Europe and beyond.

From the Adites of Arabic legends to the Titans of Greek mythology, giants were the acclaimed builders of immense megalithic stone structures whose origins lay shrouded in time. The giants with their fascinating culture seem to be the progenitors of a lost civilization and a big part of human prehistory. But where are their bones and what is left of their civilization? Does a cover-up of ancient giants exist at the Smithsonian, the Royal Academies, and within the halls of other high levels of government around the world? Besides avoiding having to rewrite the history books, what other benefits might the establishment maintain by keeping the ancient giant history of Earth a secret? The answers might be found in the same reasons full alien disclosure may never happen—fear of upsetting the religious gravy train.

As far as the media is concerned, our seven-foot-tall ancestors weren't that big of a deal because, for example, there are seven-footers playing in the NBA. And any eight-footer is immediately accused of having pituitary gland tumor issues, which those pesky ancient eight-footers must have also suffered from. And any bones ranging from nine feet and up are nothing more than exaggerations, hoaxes, or misidentified mammoth bones. Academia continues to deny the bones of ancient giants a rightful place in the annals of Earth's history while accepting no challenge that contradicts their evolutionary history of storytelling, contrary to the reports that say otherwise.

The intermingling and breeding of unknown species makes it harder to trace the exact origins of this remote and ancient race. The various shapes of certain skulls and bones can probably tell us the most about the giants, but a cover-up that's existed for hundreds of years has maintained that any relevant artifacts concerning the "giant" enigma be sequestered and hidden far away from the prying eyes of the public. Politics and history have never gotten along. One makes sure that the loser's tale is continuously rewritten while the truth traverses the ether among the selective memories of our ancestors.

Still, every once in a while the "new truth" will be challenged by the real "silent truth," which seeps through the established barriers, and threatens to challenge the accepted status quo. But when this silent truth is spoken with whistle-blowing passion by a small percentage of brave scientists and accredited academics, it is quickly diminished as crazy, impossible, a clever hoax, or—in the worst-case scenario—funding is pulled from the institution promoting it, making it nearly impossible to get any actual truth not approved of by the academic gatekeepers.

Keep in mind the discovery of pits of giant severed hands that were discovered in what was believed to be Joseph's palace in Egypt: a recent find that sheds a new light on both biblical history and the lore of ancient giants.

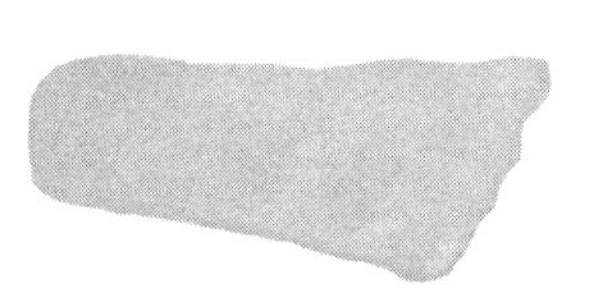

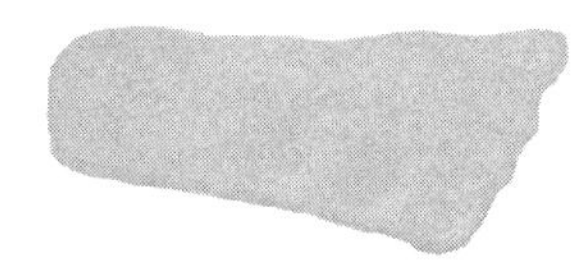

CHAPTER 1

Ancient Giants of Ireland and Britain

History, like love, is so apt to surround her heroes with an atmosphere of imaginary brightness.

James Fenimore Cooper

The giants of ancient Britain are spoken of in myths that stir the imagination, conjuring up images once written about by the bards of the royal courts. The origin of these giants is unknown, although alternative scholars point to the antediluvian lands of Atlantis.

One of the oldest poems in the English language, *Seafare,* is a first-person narrative describing the hero Theodoric's escape and battle against twelve giants who guard castle Nitgar. The poet also reflects on a walled set of immense stone ruins that were built by giants and makes a reference to the Giant's Causeway in Northern Ireland, a strange series of shaped rocks that make a pathway from Irish cliffs into the ocean (see fig. 1.1). This stone bridge was attributed to the ancient Irish giant Finn McCool, but modern academia claims it's nothing more than natural geologic basalt columns molded uniquely over time by Mother Nature.

By looking at the reported histories of the late eighteenth and nineteenth centuries, we can find a plethora of articles and newspaper

Fig. 1.1. Giant's Causeway, Northern Ireland
(photo by Chmee2, 2010)

mentions of giants being dug up all over the British and Irish landscapes. Like the mounds brimming with giant Indians found by the settlers of America as they moved West, the mounds in Ireland and England also revealed giant skeletons, dug up by eager farmers looking to reappraise their land. A twelve-foot fossilized giant was discovered by miners in County Antrim, Ireland. The Irish prospectors digging for iron ore were at a loss for words as they tried to figure out a way to bring the petrified giant to the surface. With the help of a crane they were able to raise the four-hundred-pound giant and get him on the train to Dublin for a proper evaluation.

In December 1895, the *Strand* magazine ran a picture of this fossilized giant taken at the London Rail Depot; it would be the last time the public ever saw the giant, as the story disappeared almost as quickly as it appeared. From the article we learn that the giant had six toes and had previously been exhibited in Dublin, Liverpool, and Manchester for sixpence a head.[1] A legal dispute brought it to London where it vanished from record. The fact that it was exhibited around various cities caused people to believe it might have been a hoax, and it might have been.

The Cardiff giant was exhibited around the same time and looks slightly similar to the Irish giant, even though they were discovered in different places. We do know that the Cardiff giant was indeed a hoax, admitted so by its creator, and—although there is not enough proof to claim that the Irish giant was also a hoax—to the unconvinced it's seen as an obvious act of tomfoolery.

But in 1994, a community of "Saxon giants" was discovered by prominent archaeologist Anne Finney in North Yorkshire. The skeletons were excavated from a sixth-century Saxon cemetery found hidden beneath the ruins of Thirsk Castle. One of the skeletons was that of a man more than seven feet in height. Worried about the possible ramifications of her discovery, Finney kept the artifacts hidden away in secret vaults; they were only seen by fellow academics. She even tried to halt the artifacts from being put on display by the impatient owners who kept wondering what the hell the big deal was. Cooper Harding, curator at Thirsk Museum, which houses the artifacts, says, "You can imagine the terror of the native Celtic farmers, who were quite short, when confronted by these giants."[2] The Thirsk Museum had to lobby the Yorkshire Archaeological Trust endlessly for over five years before they were finally given the artifacts back, so that they could put them on public display. However, in a strange twist of fate, the bones of the giant Saxon still remain hidden away from the public in private vaults, while the people are left to marvel at the less mysterious copper brooches and sixth-century Saxon jewelry instead.

If seven-foot giants are kept hidden, it begs the question of how many nine-, ten-, and twelve-foot giants are stored in vaults in hidden corners of the halls of so-called academia. Of course the usual excuse not to display giant bones runs along the familiar lines of respecting the remains of the dead, as if they have any respect for the still living. But they have no problem displaying the bones of Neanderthals and the alleged ape-men fossils, which they claim we evolved from millions of years ago. But no love on the same pedestal for the giant bones. I guess these bones are too damaging to their theories. Even though they admit there's a missing link, they go out of their way to suppress a possible connection in the bones of ancient giants.

It makes you take a closer look at the myths of ancient Britain. One of the earliest legends includes the world's most famous wizard, Merlin; the mystical ruins of Stonehenge; and of course ancient giants. In the 1100s the first known depiction of Stonehenge appeared in the medieval history textbook *Brut.* The sketched image shows the legendary Merlin constructing Stonehenge with the help of giants. Ancient legends claim that Stonehenge was built by Merlin who moved stones from Erin all the way to Salisbury with the help of his magical wand. Once there, both a race of giants and his wand helped in creating the megalithic solar observatory.

Stonehenge has been a mindfreak at least since it was first written about. Since the ruins have no known beginning, only time knows how many ancient kingdoms they've seen rise and fall. Academia admits Stonehenge could be as much as five thousand years old and that the complex is situated along ley lines of the earth's energy grid. In 1825 farmers discovered the bones of a seven-foot-tall person near the ruins of Stonehenge while digging to expand a barn in Humbleton.[3] But who were these seven-footers? Were they diminished survivors of that once mighty race of giants?

Some historians claim these were either the Phoenicians or Hittites or perhaps even the distant relatives of the Mer and Martu clans, representing the "The Amorite Giants"[4] of the Old Testament and the Torah. These were the giants of modern-day Syria, Libya, and Palestine, known as the sons of "Anak,"[5] whose name comes from the Akkadian word for "tin" or "tarnish," implying that the Anak had serious riches, and they did. They were the ones that supplied the gold for King Solomon's temples. Where they got this gold remains a mystery, but since the Phoenicians were renowned for their seafaring mastery, possible guesses range from Wales to Australia and even as far away as the ancient gold mines in northern Arizona. Despite being a once mighty force, it is doubtful Phoenicians had any hand in building Stonehenge unless it was done by their twelve-foot-tall Anak ancestors.

In Norfolk, a giant ax was discovered in the beach below Beeston Hill, Sheringham, and reported by *Nature Magazine* in 1935:

> An altogether remarkable and gigantic hand-axe, discovered embedded, by Mr. J. P. T. Burchell . . . the implement measures in its greatest length 15J inches, in greatest width 6J inches, in greatest thickness 5J inches. Its weight is approximately 14 lbs. It was derived originally from the base of the Cromer Forest bed, which rests upon the surface of the chalk. The implementiferous bed runs in beneath the Forest Bed strata and the glacial deposits which form the cliff, some 200 ft. in height. The material of the axe is of flint, the colour of the flaked surfaces being jet black . . . the numerous specimens discovered in the basement bed, belonging to the early Pleistocene epoch, are as highly specialised as are those of any later prehistoric period and represent a very definite and necessary stage in implemental development. No adequate explanation of the purpose which the gigantic size of the Sheringham axe could serve has been offered.[6]

The dig produced two mint-condition giant axes and a cleaver awl dating from the Lower Paleolithic era, which lasted from 600,000 to 250,000 BCE in Britain. The bones found in the same strata crumbled to dust when exposed to air.

Around the year 1660, on the banks of the Cor in Northumberland, England, local floods unearthed a giant skeleton with a thigh bone over six feet long.[7] The skull and remaining teeth were described as monstrous and kept in the possession of the Earl of Derwentwater, who was known for his underground ritual orgies in the late 1600s. One of the bones made it to the Old George Inn in New Castle, where it was displayed before being purchased by the proprietor of the Keswick

Museum. It was redisplayed as the rib of the giant Cor[8] before disappearing in the backroom vaults in the 1980s.

The *Milwaukee Sentinel* reported about three ten-footers discovered in Ireland in 1914:

> An interesting discovery was recently made in Ireland. During the course of some excavating work two men unearthed three human skeletons. One was entire and measured eighteen inches from the crown of the head to the chin. The leg bones are abnormally large and altogether the skeleton appeared to be that of a person ten feet high. The teeth were large, and the remains are supposed to date from a prehistoric age.[9]

The Great Orme Copper Mine, which dates to the Bronze Age, is located near the coastal town of Llandudno in North Wales. More than seventeen hundred tons of copper are known to have been removed from the mine along with over twenty-five thousand ax heads, including a massive sixty-four-pound sledgehammer found by archaeologists deep in the mine. The nine-foot-long handle would be heavy enough to lift without the ax head attached. To swing it with the sixty-four-pound hammer on top would require an impossible amount of strength that not even a juiced Bruce Banner could pull off. More ten-foot-tall giant skeletons[10] were discovered in Dysart, Ireland, after a group of workers broke through three separate stone graves in 1914. Although one of the skeletons was entirely intact, nothing more was ever reported on the matter.

In 1951 the *St. Petersburg Times* reported on a set of giant skeletons unearthed after the mounds that housed them were destroyed by farmers in the Four Knocks, County Meath, area of Ireland:

> Irish archaeologists have unearthed traces of a bygone race of "supermen."The findings may provide scientific substantiation for legends of a race of seven-foot giants who inhabited the island of

Hibernia (Ireland) in its golden age, long before the dawn of history. In a prehistoric burial chamber dating back to 2000 BC, they found human skeletons which tower head and shoulders over modern man stretched in slab-topped graves with offerings of food and ornaments beside them. Most are around seven feet in height, of extraordinary width of shoulder and massive bone construction. . . . In the remote rural areas, old folks still point out where, according to legend, the great Irish Warrior Cushalainn crushed the imprint of his mighty foot in the rocky bank of the river after a colossal leap across the raging torrent. Throughout the nation, story tellers relate similar feats by other Irish warriors and heroes of the island's golden past. Now, for the first time, what may be concrete evidence has come to hand to support the legends of a race of supermen.[11]

Fig. 1.2. *Sigurd Battles an Irish Giant,* Henry Justice (*The Crimson Fairy Book,* London, New York, Longmans, Green and Co., 1903)

Medieval writer Geoffrey of Monmouth became one of the most famous men in Europe when his *History of the First Kings of Britain* was published in the year 1136. A collection of ancient tales and pagan folklores, his book became the bestseller of its time and served as a critical backbone of English and European history until being written off and derided as mere fantasy after the rise of Darwinism. Geoffrey of Monmouth's medieval bestseller contains the legends of Welsh and Irish tales, which he claims to have translated into Latin, from older books that he received from an Oxford Archdeacon.

Unfortunately these earlier books haven't survived, leaving some scholars to assume that Geoffrey made the whole history up as a sort of unintentional prelude to the future works of Tolkien. Despite being written off by mainstream academia, some historians have claimed that *History of the Kings of Britain* is a genuine history of ancient Britain. It even shares the same tales of ancient giants that can be found in the histories from all over the world, a common theme since the beginning of the written word.

Geoffrey's *History* begins with an introduction telling us that Britain was once known as Albion and home to an ancient race of giants. The mighty Trojan warrior Brutus was told by the goddess Diana that Albion was the land his exiled peoples, left over from the Trojan War, would settle after defeating the giants that resided there. With little worry, Brutus and his platoon of warriors and former Trojan slaves washed ashore and quickly laid waste to the remaining giants of Albion. The island was renamed Britain in honor of their giant-slaying leader, Brutus, and their settlement called New Troy by the River Thames would eventually be known as the great city of London.

Geoffrey of Monmouth describes a legendary battle that took place during the siege of Albion, in which the giant Gogmagog was thrown off the cliff by the Cornish strongman Corineus. Gogmagog was the last of the giants and remained a popular figure in the oldest works of Welsh and Gaelic folklores. The place where Gogmagog fell to his death was known as Goëmagot's Leap, and was believed to be on

Fig. 1.3. *Combat between Brutus's Troops and the Giants of Albion,* artist unknown (from Geoffrey's *Historia Regum Britannae,* in Harley MS 1808, fol. 30. Held and digitized by the British Library.)

Lambhay Hill in the historic Barbican district of Plymouth. Legendary seventeenth-century English poet, scribe, and historian John Milton also wrote a *History of Britain* in which he gives this account:

> The Island, not yet Britain, but Albion, was in a manner desert and inhospitable, kept only by a remnant of Giants, whose excessive Force and Tyrannie had consumed the rest. Them Brutus destroies, and to his people divides the land, which, with some reference to his own name, he thenceforth calls Britain. To Corineus, Cornwall, as now we call it, fell by lot; the rather by him lik't, for that the hugest Giants in Rocks and Caves were said to lurk still there; which kind of Monsters to deal with was his old exercise. And heer, with leave bespok'n to recite a grand fable, though dignify'd by our best Poets: While Brutus, on a certain Festival day, solemnly kept on that

Fig. 1.4. *Gogmagog: The Giant of Guildhall,* one of two wooden figures displayed in the Guildhall in London, carved by Captain Richard Saunders in 1709, replacing earlier wicker-and-pasteboard effigies, which were traditionally carried in the Lord Mayor's Show. They represent the legendary characters of Gogmagog and Corineus, but were later known as Gog and Magog. Both figures were destroyed during the London Blitz, 1940; new figures were carved in 1953. (F.W. Fairholt, *Gog and Magog: The Giants in Guildhall, London,* 1859, 14.)

> shore where he first landed (Totnes), was with the People in great jollity and mirth, a crew of these savages, breaking in upon them, began on the sudden another sort of Game than at such a meeting was expected. But at length by many hands overcome, Gogmagog, the hugest, in hight twelve cubits, is reserved alive; that with him Corineus, who desired nothing more, might try his strength, whom in a Wrestle the Giant catching aloft, with a terrible hugg broke three of his Ribs: Nevertheless Corineus, enraged, heaving him up by main force, and on his shoulders bearing him to the next high rock, threw him hedlong all shatter'd into the sea, and left his name on the cliff, called ever since Langoemagog, which is to say, the Giant's Leap.[12]

During the coronation of Queen Elizabeth I in 1558, an effigy of the Albion giant Gogmagog was made and paraded about in honor of the ancient British giant; this practice continued in the Lord Mayor's

Show for centuries after. Captain Richard Saunders carved a new effigy from pine in 1709 and displayed the carving of the ancient giant in the Guildhall until an air raid destroyed it in 1940.

In the works of Irish mythology, like the *Lebor Gabála Érenn* (Book of Invasions), Gogmagog was considered to be an ancestor of the mighty Partholón, a leader of the first group of giants that colonized Ireland after the Great Flood. These post-flood colonizers were known as the Fomorians, who, according to Irish legend, were a seafaring race of abominable giants and monsters. Some Fomorians were giants with cyclopic traits while others displayed different sets of eyes and extremities like some of the Hindu gods of India.

The most famous Fomorian leader was King Balor, who possessed an eye in the middle of his forehead, along with an extra eye in the back of his head. Balor is known in Irish mythology as the god of death and destruction. According to legend, Balor obtained his magical eyes after being caught spying on some Druid shamans, who then spilled an enchanted elixir in Balor's eyes. Balor's eye then became an evil weapon that eviscerated islands and caused fear and dread throughout the emerald isles. Could this "eye" have been some sort of lost ancient technology from before the flood? In Irish professor Alan Ward's *Myths of the Gods: Structures in Irish Mythology,* Balor's "eye" is described as being some sort of machine:

> It was always covered with seven cloaks to keep it cool. He took the cloaks off one by one. At the first, ferns began to wither. At the second, grass began to redden. At the third, wood and trees began to heat up. At the fourth, smoke came out of wood and trees. At the fifth, everything got red hot. At the sixth . . . at the seventh, the whole land caught fire.[13]

Because he had a giant-sized eye of destruction, Balor came to realize that keeping his eyes closed was the only suitable way of living in peace. It took four other Fomorian giants to help keep Balor's eye closed.

Fig. 1.5. *Dana—The Mother Goddess of the Tuatha Dé Danann*, Genzoman (Deviantart.com, 2009)

The ancient Irish tribe known as the Tuatha de Danann was another post-flood group that rivaled the Fomorians with their magic and seemingly lost technology. They were described in the *Battles at Mag Tuired* as:

1. The Tuatha De Danann were in the northern islands of the world, studying occult lore and sorcery, druidic arts and witchcraft and magical skill, until they surpassed the sages of the pagan arts.
2. They studied occult lore and secret knowledge and diabolic arts in four cities: Falias, Gorias, Murias, and Findias.
3. From Falias was brought the Stone of Fal which was located in Tara. It used to cry out beneath every king that would take Ireland.
4. From Gorias was brought the spear which Lug had. No battle was ever sustained against it, or against the man who held it in his hand.
5. From Findias was brought the sword of Nuadu. No one ever escaped from it once it was drawn from its deadly sheath, and no one could resist it.
6. From Murias was brought the Dagda's cauldron. No company ever went away from it unsatisfied.
7. There were four wizards in those four cities. Morfesa was in Falias; Esras was in Gorias; Uiscias was in Findias; Semias was in Murias. Those are the four poets from whom the Tuatha De learned occult lore and secret knowledge.
8. The Tuatha De then made an alliance with the Fomoire, and Balor the grandson of Net gave his daughter Ethne to Cian the son of Dian Cecht. And she bore the glorious child, Lug.
9. The Tuatha De came with a great fleet to Ireland to take it by force from the Fir Bolg. Upon reaching the territory of Corcu Belgatan (which is Conmaicne Mara today), they at once burned their boats so that they would not think of fleeing to them. The

> smoke and the mist which came from the ships filled the land and the air which was near them. For that reason it has been thought that they arrived in clouds of mist.[14]

It appears that this semi-divine ancient Irish tribe even possessed some spaceships and other far-out types of lost technology usually attributed to the gods. Settling the lands of Northern Ireland, the Tuatha de Danann would eventually breed with the Fomorians, which, according to Celtic lore, begat the first race of the Faoladh, more commonly known as werewolves.

CHAPTER 2

Ancient Giants of France and Spain

The first duty of a man is to think for himself.

José Martí

GIANT GAULS AND GARGANTUA OF FRANCE

In 101 BCE, Roman general Gaius Marius secured two important military victories at the battles of the Aquae Sextiae and the battle of Vercellae. It was the first time in nearly a hundred years that the Romans had been able to defeat the tribes of giant Gaul warriors from southern France. During his expeditions north of Rome, Caesar continued to find various tribes of giant warriors all the way up into England. After witnessing a few battles against these burly long-haired warriors, Caesar assumed they were impossible to defeat without a massive army and advanced forms of weaponry. Diodorus, the Roman historian, described their frightening presence: "The Gauls are tall in stature, with rippling muscles . . . they are terrifying in aspect and their voices are deep and altogether harsh."[1]

The giants of France were part of that larger Gaul empire that stretched into Germany and most of Europe. Eventually these ripped giant warriors that inhabited the coastal areas of the North Atlantic began to die off. As the industrial world formed, their exploits became nothing more than Druid fantasy. Then, in 1894, some of their giant kin were discovered in Montpellier, France, after workmen digging a water reservoir discovered large human skulls measuring thirty-two inches in circumference.[2] Digging further down, they found bones of gigantic proportions, which they sent to the Paris Academy for a more detailed study. A scientist involved in the study believed the bones belonged to a race of men nearly fifteen feet high. Unfortunately these bones have since disappeared.

Montpellier is a few miles south of Castelnau-le-Lez, home of the legendary Castelnau giant. This eleven-foot-tall giant was known all throughout central France as being a fierce cannibalistic warlord before he died of old age and ill health. But the continual displaying of his giant eleven-foot-tall skeleton in the foyer of Castelnau-le-Lez made sure that his once feared exploits continued to haunt the locals. His legend soon slipped into obscurity and his bones vanished as the march of time moved on and the castle slipped into ruin. Then in the misty winter of 1890, French anthropologist Georges Vacher de Lapouge excavated a Bronze Age cemetery on the castle grounds that revealed three giant bone fragments. His findings were later published in the French journal *La Nature.* Because the bones were discovered at the bottom of a Bronze Age burial, he figured them to be at the very least of the Neolithic era. Vacher de Lapouge describes the bones in *La Nature:*

> I think it unnecessary to note that these bones are undeniably human, despite their enormous size . . . the volumes of the bones were more than double the normal pieces to which they correspond. Judging by the usual intervals of anatomical points, they also involve lengths almost double. . . . The subject would have been a likely size of 3m, 50.[3]

Three and a half meters is roughly eleven feet five inches tall, a fearful height that lends credence to the old tales of the Castelnau giant spun by the locals of Castelnau-le-Lez. Since their discovery by Vacher de Lapouge the giant bones were studied in the early 1890s by prominent scientists at the University of Montpellier's School of Medicine, who all concluded they belonged to a "very tall race."[4] A recent inquiry into these historically important bones has fallen on deaf ears, as neither the University of Montpellier nor the current residents near Castelnau-le-Lez have any idea about what has happened to them or their current whereabouts.

Nearby in Vichy, France, a set of handprints measuring over fourteen inches long were discovered imprinted in clay. This ancient set of handprints could have only belonged to somebody at least ten feet tall. You can see them for yourself at the museum of Glozel in a farming provence that has yielded many curious artifacts since the 1920s. Whether these "Glozel artifacts"[5] are real or part of an elaborate hoax is still up for debate.

Fig. 2.1. Glozel artifacts at the museum in Ferrières-sur-Sichon, Allier, France, in 1920 (Bibliothèque nationale de France)

However, one of the most popular illustrated books of all time is the sixteenth-century French tale of *Gargantua and Pantagruel*. Written by Rabelais and first published in 1534, the five-volume epic was inspired by the French legends of ancient giants.

That these were more than legends is indicated by discoveries made in the nineteenth and twentieth centuries. In 1935, road workers in Gap, France, unearthed a cemetery of giant skeletons, the largest being eight feet seven inches in height.[6] In Reims, a thirteen-foot skeleton was unearthed by a farmer in 1851.

The *Miami News* reported on the giant discoveries workers made in Paris in 1918:

> Paris.—Military prisoners digging at Vandancourt, near Paris, discovered a tomb thousands of years old, of unpolished slabs of stone, filled with human bones of gigantic proportions. The skulls were oval and the teeth resembled those of a horse. Archaeologists say the tomb dates back to the copper age.[7]

A more detailed report emerged in 1933, which spoke about more giant bones being unearthed in the Paris vicinity. The *Freeport Journal Standard* out of Illinois reports:

> Skeletons of Seven foot tall giants Neolithic
>
> Paris.—Paul Lemoine, the Director of the Paris Museum of Natural History, M. Lantier, curator of the archaeological museum of Saint-Germain-en-Laye, Professor Rivet and other savants, have visited the tomb and all agreed it is of sufficient interest for excavation work to be continued with renewed effort. . . . Eight seven-foot skeletons were brought to light beneath a huge monolith, weighing more than four tons. A number of the bones were burnt, indicating that the bodies had been burned before burial, and little was found around them, save a few flint arrows and spearheads, which lead to the belief that the persons buried were not of very high social caste.[8]

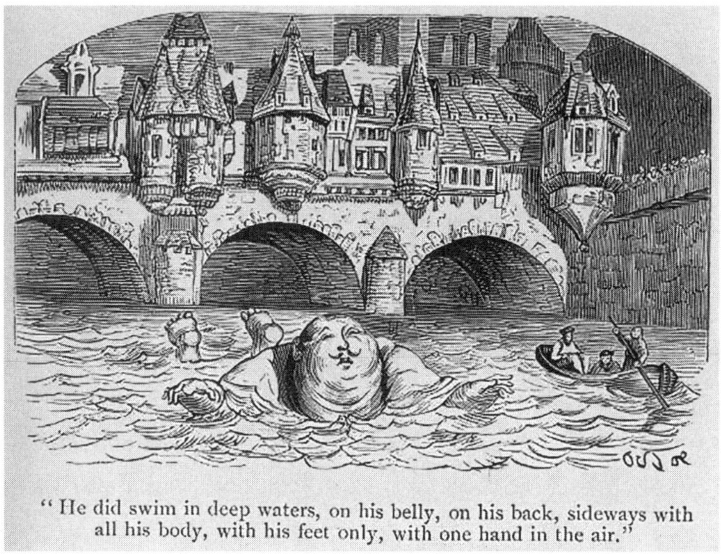

"He did swim in deep waters, on his belly, on his back, sideways with all his body, with his feet only, with one hand in the air."

Fig. 2.2. Illustration for *Gargantua and Pantagruel*, Gustave Dore (1873)

Ancient French Giants Exhumed

Gap, France—(AP)—Road menders near here uncovered the cemetery of some ancient tribe of giants. The skeletons, one of which measured 8 feet 7 inches, lay in a sarcophagi formed of flat stones.

Fig. 2.3. "Ancient French Giants Exhumed" (*Evening Tribune*, August 16, 1935)

Skeleton of a Giant.—Recently a gentleman in the neighborhood of the ancient city of Reims, in making an excavation for some purpose, discovered a human skeleton, well preserved, which was four metres (13 ft.) long.

Fig. 2.4. "13-Foot-Long Skeleton of Reims" (*Oswego Commercial Times*, August 8, 1851)

Giants of Prehistoric France.

In a prehistoric cemetery recently uncovered at Montpellier, France, while workmen were excavating a waterworks reservoir, human skulls were found measuring 28, 31 and 32 inches in circumference. The bones which were found with the skulls were also of gigantic proportions. These relics were sent to the Paris academy, and a learned "savant," who lectured on the find, says that they belonged to a race of men between 10 and 15 feet in height.

Fig. 2.5. "Giants of Prehistoric France" (*Oelwein Register*, November 8, 1894)

These large out-of-place bones prompted a meeting of the Prehistoric Society of France, where prominent scientists and historians poured over the French historical records of ancient giants. It was enough to convince them that a mysterious race of giants had indeed once called the lands of modern-day France their home. This was especially so in the summer of 1935 after archaeologists unearthed another cemetery in southeast France that was home to "some ancient tribe of giants. . . . The skeletons, one of which is 8 feet 7 inches."[9]

More of these giant skeletons from an unknown race prone to sleeping in stone coffins had been found in the Grenoble area of southern France in 1930. Workers digging a new road found fourteen stone coffins buried more than twelve feet in the ground as reported by a correspondent of the *London Daily Mail* on location in France. The slate coffins were of a prehistoric era, and the skeletons of fourteen gigantic men were revealed to have been buried there. The skulls and jawbones were double the size[10] of the individuals investigating them. Most of the bones disintegrated when exposed to air, and the whereabouts of the remaining bones or coffins is not known. In the ancient French city of Reims, a well-preserved thirteen-foot-long skeleton of a giant was unearthed by farmers in 1851. It has since disappeared.[11]

Another legendary giant was the Germanic king Teutobochus of the Teutons, whose bones were unearthed in southeastern France, causing much fanfare and hype in 1613. In 1869, W. A. Seaver recalled the event:

> In times more modern (1613), some masons digging near the ruins of a castle in Dauphiné, in a field which by tradition had long been called "The Giant's Field," at a depth of 18 feet discovered a brick tomb 30 feet long, 12 feet wide, and 8 feet high, on which was a gray stone with the words "Theutobochus Rex" cut thereon. When the tomb was opened they found a human skeleton entire, 25½ feet long, 10 feet wide across the shoulders, and 5 feet deep from the breast to the back. His teeth were about the size of an ox's foot, and his shin-bone measured 4 feet in length.[12]

Despite the tomb and a full skeleton, modern science proclaimed the bones to be nothing more than those of a mastodon. Even still, it's no surprise that the original giant bones of King Teutobochus have also gone missing.

SPANISH GIANTS, FROM THE CANARY ISLAND GUANCHES TO THE BASQUE JENTILS

Spain, France's neighbor to the south, also has a prehistoric conundrum concerning ancient giants. The north of Spain has a rich tradition of giants roaming around in the days of yore. Although most pagan traditions, including tales of witches and giants, were outlawed by the church, enough of their lore survived to be orally passed down and recorded when the printing press finally came around. In the Catalonia regions ancient giants still star in many local festivals and parades, as do the "gentile giants," as they are known in the Basque country, where folktales about them are still told to children. Basque mythology calls the giants *jentil,* a word similar to the Hebrew *gentile* (non-Jew). The megalithic stone wonders left behind in Spain were attributed to the giants, although very few have survived and most history books rarely mention them.

However, there is an underground megalithic cave system in Antequera, Spain (see figs. 2.6, 2.7, and 2.8). The very name of the region actually means "ancient," validating the immense age of the mysteries found there. The Cueva de Menga dolmens complex[13] is one of the largest stone structures in Europe, running more than eighty-five feet underground. It's an archaeological wonder containing at least thirty megaliths, with an average weight each of at least one hundred tons, and quarried at the very least eight miles away.

And the world's oldest known cave art created by Neanderthals over forty thousand years ago can be found inside the El Castillo cave in Cantabria, Spain (see fig. 2.9).[14]

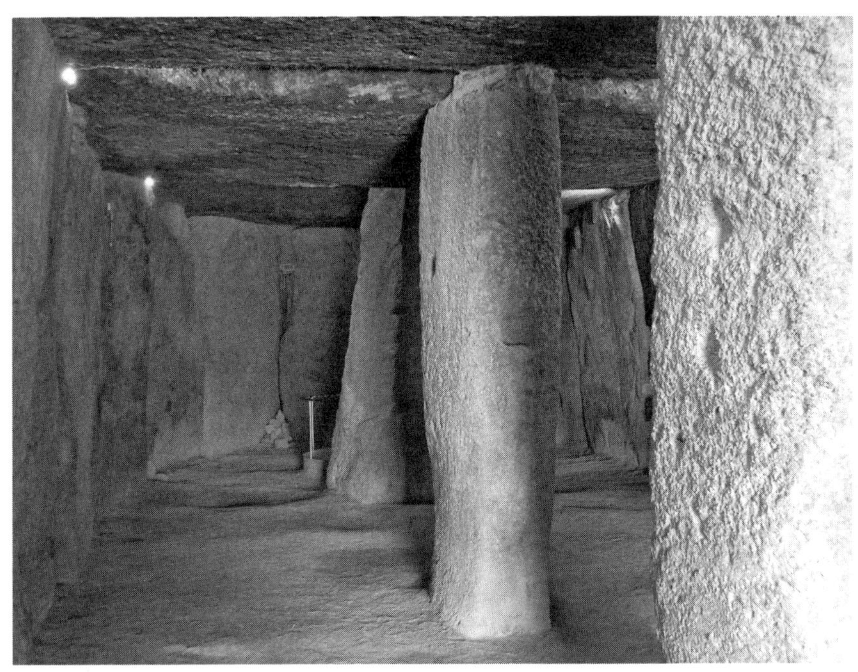

Fig. 2.6. Antequera's Menga Dolmen 1
(photo by Andrzej Otrębski, 2010)

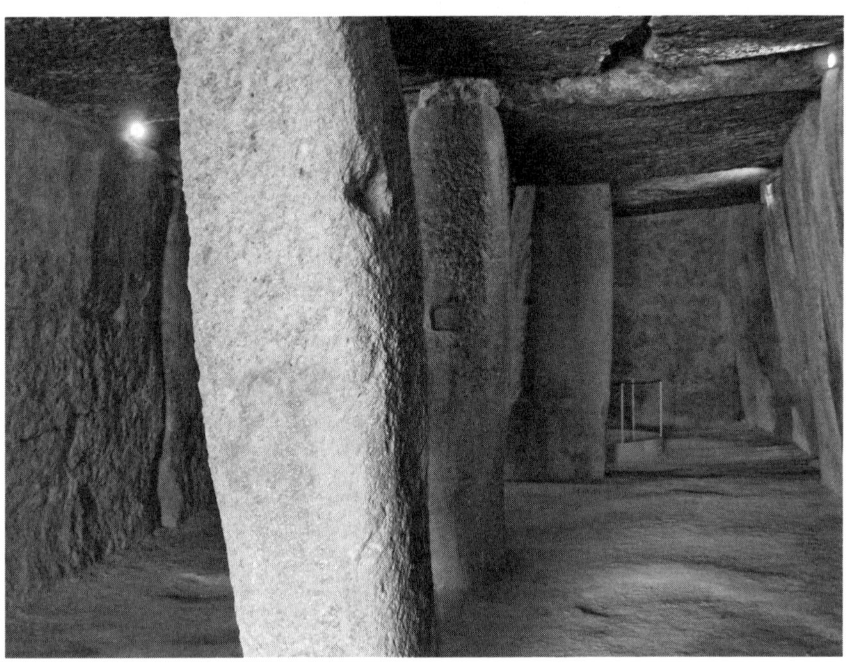

Fig. 2.7. Antequera's Menga Dolmen 2
(photo by Andrzej Otrębski, 2010)

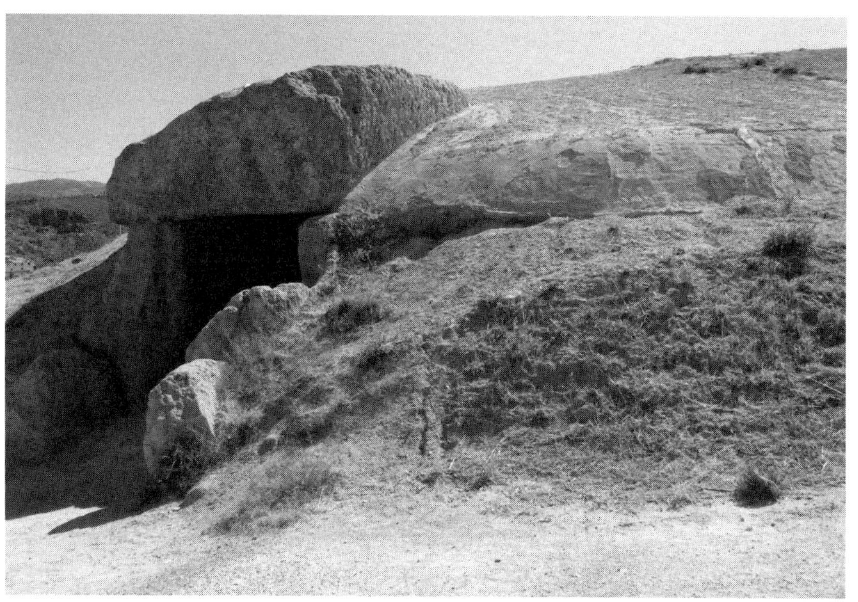

Fig. 2.8. Entrance to Antequera's Menga Dolmen
(photo by Andrzej Otrębski, 2010)

Fig. 2.9. Cave of El Castillo in Spain, home to the world's oldest artwork, believed to be at least 40,800 years old
(photo by Gabinete de Prensa del Gobierno de Cantabria, 2008)

The megalithic ruins of Los Millares are another series of ancient ruins attributed to giants by the locals but claimed by academia as being the results of a more primitive Neolithic tribe. You know, because primitives had such an easy time moving one-hundred-ton megalithic blocks around with their archaic skill sets. And never mind the giant femur bone found at the megalithic dolmen site of Oren, high in the Catalan Pyrenees in 1917.[15]

In the Lleida Pyrenees a church restoration unearthed a ten-foot-tall giant skeleton complete with an iron nail drilled into his skull.[16] A few mountains over, more giant skeletons were unearthed during another church-inspired archaeological dig, along with giant skulls found in the remaining plunders after the falling of Castile Medinaceli in the 1800s.[17] The Visigothic church Marialba also revealed giant skeletons as big as those bones found during renovations at a church twenty miles away in Girona.[18] In Valencia, a gigantic twenty-two-foot-tall skeleton was discovered by farmers in 1705. A giant skull was also found in the vicinity; the skull was apparently big enough to hold a bushel of corn.[19]

In the Spanish-controlled territories of the Canary Islands, the mysterious Guanches were an ancient race of blond-haired, blue-eyed giants whose origins were unknown. Despite being associated with Spain, the Canary Islands are situated off the coast of Western Sahara, Africa, and usually visited after hitching a boat ride from its tiny port city at Dakhla, which makes the existence of giant blond natives off the west coast of Africa even more peculiar. Soviet historian B. L. Bogayevsky claims the Guanches were the ancient survivors of the drowned Atlantis. Bogayevsky writes, "It is most probable that parts of the African continent broke away in the early Neolithic, giving rise to quite large islands. A new island, consequently, lay in the 'Atlantic' in front of the 'Pillars of Hercules.' This island, whose size popular fantasy could always exaggerate was, possibly, the Atlantis of Plato."[20]

As for the Guanches, reports from the late 1890s describe them to "have been strong and handsome, and of extraordinary agility of movement, of remarkable courage and of loyal disposition; but they showed

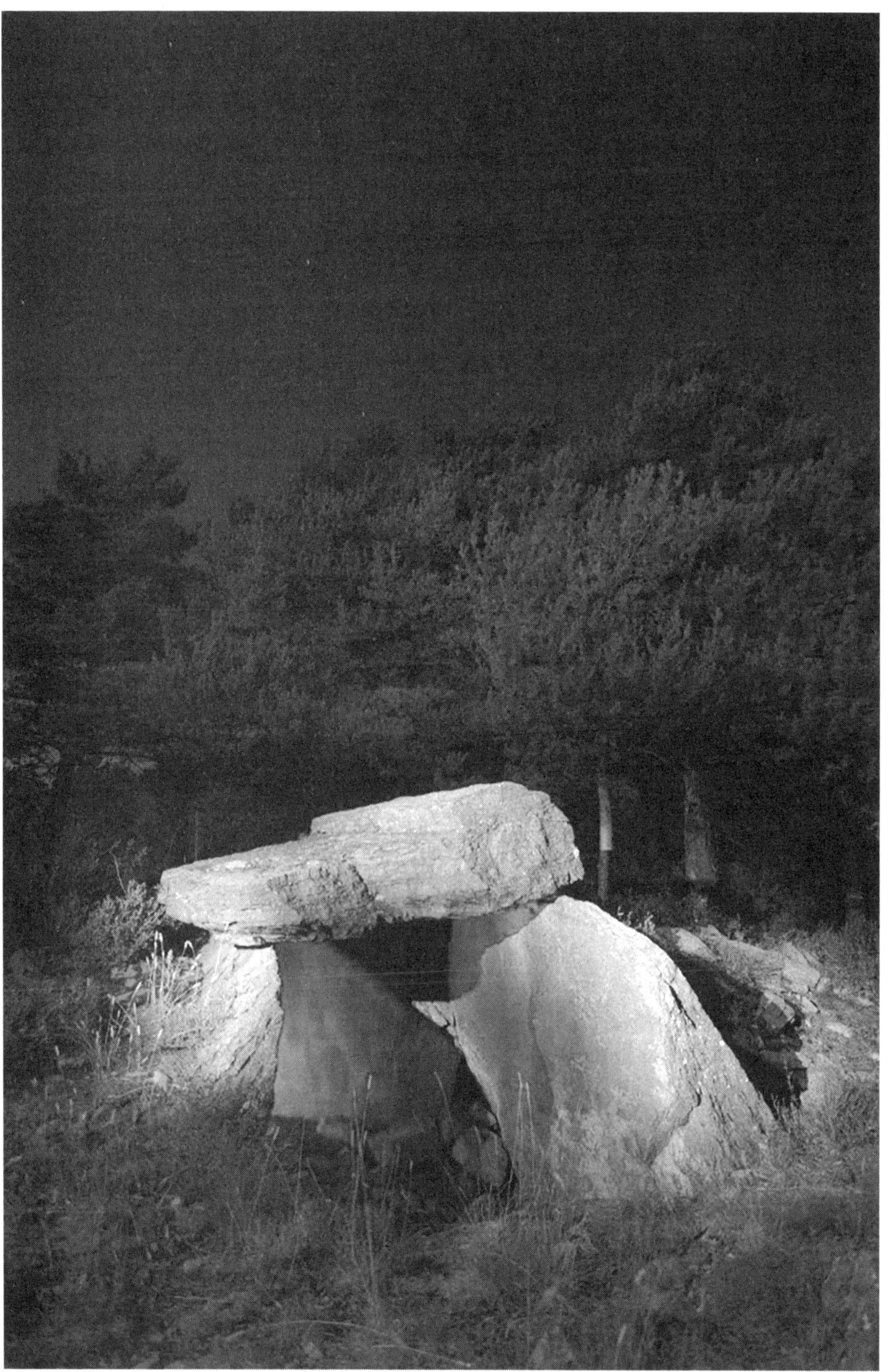

Fig. 2.10. Dolmen of Oren, Prullans, Spain
(photo by Victor Gavalda, 2012)

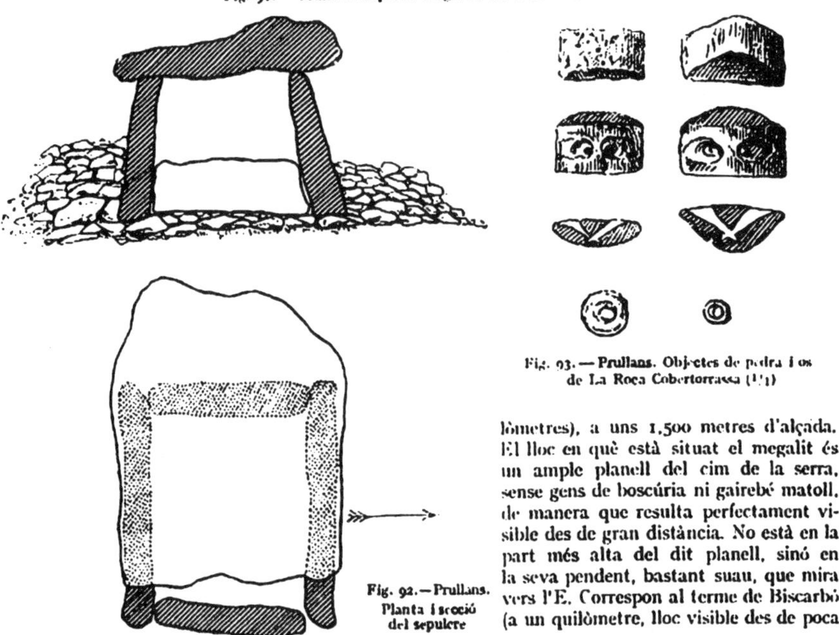
Fig. 91. — Prullans. Sepulcre megalític La Roca Cobertorrassa

Fig. 92.—Prullans. Planta i secció del sepulcre

Fig. 93. — Prullans. Objectes de pedra i os de La Roca Cobertorrassa (1/1)

lòmetres), a uns 1.500 metres d'alçada. El lloc en què està situat el megalit és un ample planell del cim de la serra, sense gens de boscúria ni gairebé matoll, de manera que resulta perfectament visible des de gran distància. No està en la part més alta del dit planell, sinó en la seva pendent, bastant suau, que mira vers l'E. Correspon al terme de Biscarbó (a un quilòmetre, lloc visible des de poca

Fig. 2.11. The Dolmen of Oren
(Institut destudis catalans seccio historico arqueologica anuari, 1921–1926, vol. vii, p.48)

the credulity of children and the simple directness of shepherds."[21] The Guanches of the 1400s were even taller, impressing the first wave of Spanish explorers who wrote about their gigantic stature and the endless amount of brute strength they seemed to possess, claiming, "They ran as fast as horses and could leap over a pole held between two men five or six feet high; they could climb the highest mountains and jump the deepest ravines."[22] The Guanches also lived in stone houses and apparently were responsible for the megalithic dolmens and conical mounds found scattered throughout the islands.

Giants were also prominent figures in the legends of the Basque regions of southern France and northern Spain. Ancient Spaniards known as the Iberians have been a part of the Basque region for at least seven thousand years. With a language not related to any other

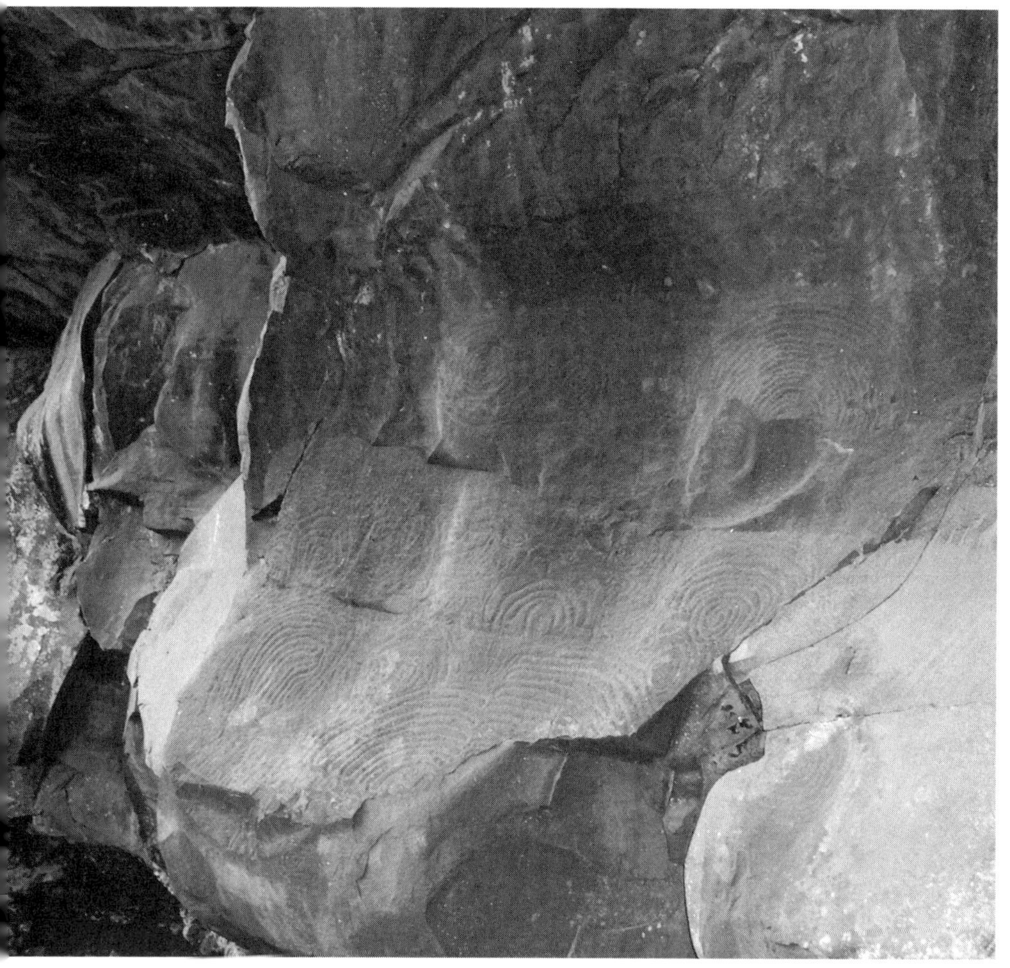

Fig. 2.12. Guanche engravings, Canary Islands (photo by Luc Viatour, www.Lucnix.be, 2005)

Indo-European language and a genetic structure containing the rarest of blood types, these Iberians have always been considered a mysterious people. This ancient Basque race also has a detailed history of giants within their folkloric origin stories. According to the Basques, these giants were a race of tall people who loved building massive megalithic stone structures (see fig. 2.13). Eventually the giants died off and the remaining ones took to the secluded forests where they were written about by future generations as the giant "wild men" of the trees.

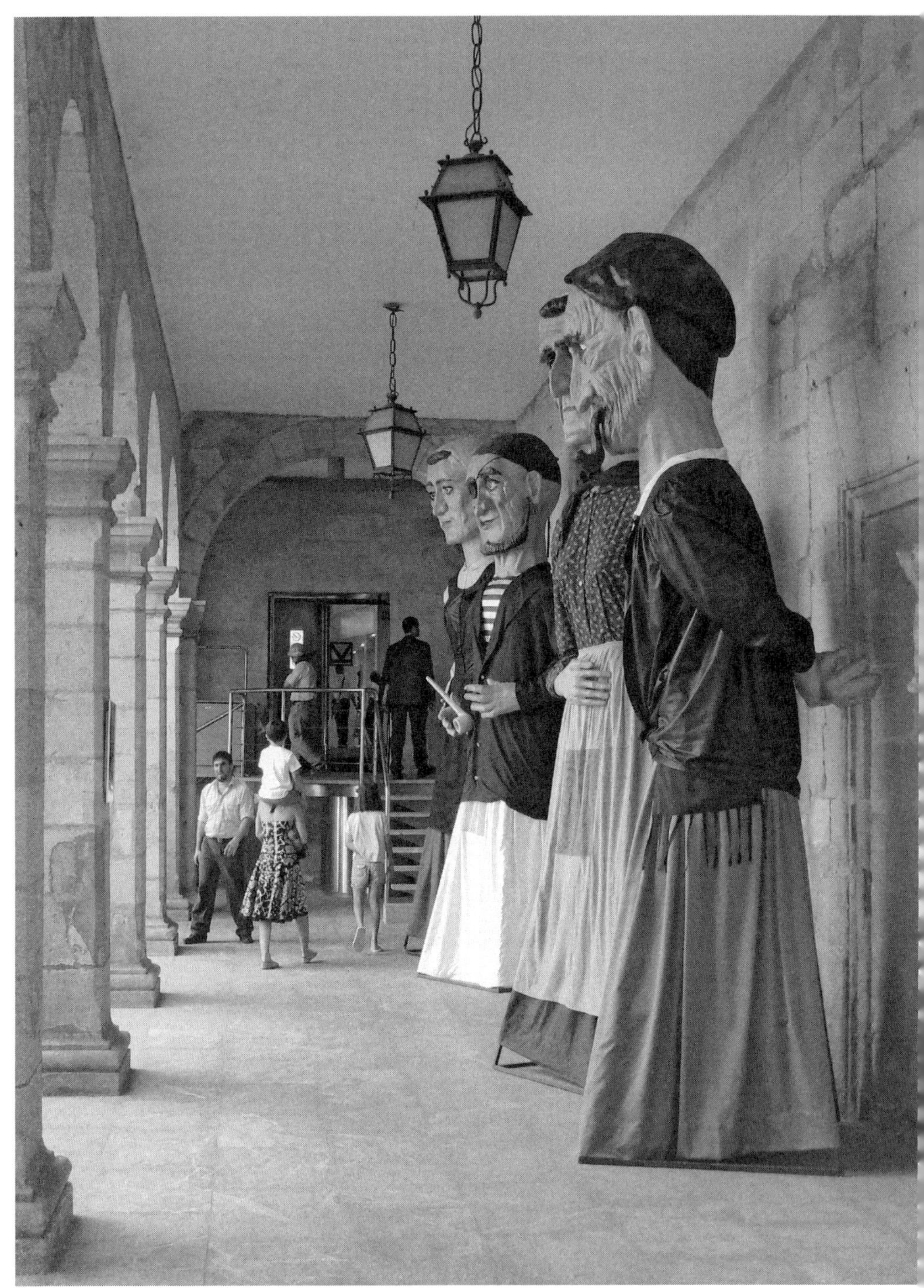

Fig. 2.13. Portable figures of giants exhibited at the cloister of the former Saint John's Convent, currently the Basque Museum, in Bilbao (photo by Javier Mediavilla Ezquibela, 2008)

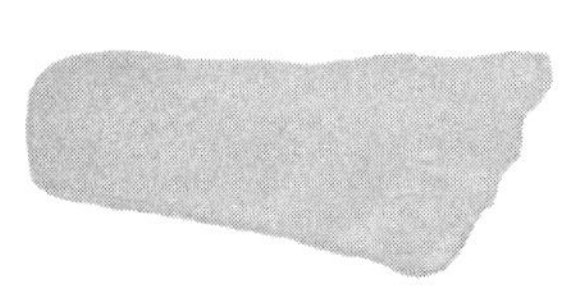

CHAPTER 3

Ancient Giants of Italy and Germany

One of the saddest lessons of history is this: If we've been bamboozled long enough, we tend to reject any evidence of the bamboozle. We're no longer interested in finding out the truth. The bamboozle has captured us. It's simply too painful to acknowledge, even to ourselves, that we've been taken. Once you give a charlatan power over you, you almost never get it back.

Carl Sagan

ITALY'S MANY TOMBS OF GIANTS

In the annals of Roman history the so-called Crisis of the Third Century (238–235 BCE) was kicked off by a giant emperor named Maximinus Thrax. Just as his name suggests, Thrax was a badass, a soldier who fought his way up from the bottom and made his way to the top of the Roman scrap heap, slowly destroying its legacy in the process. Thrax was bold, brutish, ugly as a caveman, and huge, with some sources claiming him to be over eight feet tall. He was a possible ancestor of the giant Gauls that Julius Caesar fought in France. Coins of the era depict Thrax with a massive head and the facial and skull features of a Cro-Magnon man. The historian Herodianus says that Thrax easily outwrestled and outboxed the best Roman and Greek athletes and that Thrax's physique was unmatched in shape and size throughout the entire known world.

Thrax was a legendary commander who marched his troops deep into Germany, leading to the death of the current emperor and his family near Mainz. Thrax was now the new emperor and headed back to overthrow Rome and declare himself the new Caesar. But the giant and his troops soon became dissatisfied with their plans as weeks passed by without them being able to break the barriers of Rome's impenetrable gates. Soon they were starved and dehydrated. The troops ambushed Thrax and his son in their sleep. Thrax's giant head was cut off and posted high on a stake as a warning to those entering Rome.[1]

In the Lombardy region of northern Italy, the bones of an eight-foot-tall giant were found at the Castello di Trezzo d'Adda in 1976.[2] Related to the royal lineage of the giant king Poto who ruled Lombardy circa 700 BCE, this skeleton—who was too big for the coffin he was found in—now resides in an air-conditioned vault at an archaeological museum in Milan. His giant bones are kept hidden away and not visible to the public, which seems to be the norm when dealing with giant artifacts, continuing the establishment attempts to keep the public in the dark about their existence.

A similar discovery was made by the English captain James Allen in the summer of 1807, near the Port of Girgenti, Sicily. After skin diving for conch in the cool bay, Captain Allen and his crew went on a hike uphill to an ancient sulfur mine where they descended more than one hundred feet down, only to discover a stone sarcophagi sticking out of one of the dynamited walls. After getting the sarcophagi out of the rocks and opened up, they were astonished to find the skeletal remains of an ancient, almost eleven-foot-tall giant.[3]

The Barma Grande cave near the Italian border with France revealed a giant skeleton some seven and a half feet in length with one

Fig. 3.1. The Girgenti 10'6" giant discovered by Captain James Allen (as illustrated in 1807)

of the femur bones measuring an impressive twenty-two inches long.[4] In the Sicilian capital of Palermo, a giant skeleton was unearthed by a crew of hardworking quarry men in 1516. The skeleton was said to be over thirty feet high and with a wingspan at a stunning nine feet seven inches from each point of the shoulders. A large bluish stone ax, nearly three feet long and almost ten inches thick, and weighing over sixty pounds, was found next to the sleeping giant. But in 1622 the mighty skeleton was burned into ash by a mob concerned over the Black Death spreading through Palermo (see fig. 3.2). The remaining skull was described by medieval historian Abbe Ferregus as being larger than a basket that holds a full bushel and with a jaw brimming with over sixty-four teeth confined in double rows.[5]

Eight-foot giant skeletons have also been discovered on Sardinia Island off the coast of Italy, home to a series of ancient megalithic grave sites known as the "Tombs of the Giants" (see figs. 3.3–3.6).

Fig. 3.2. Dolmen and tomb of a giant in Sicily
(photo by Stefania Zeta, 2014)

Fig. 3.3. Tomb of a giant in Siddi, Sardinia
(photo by Gianni Careddu, 2016)

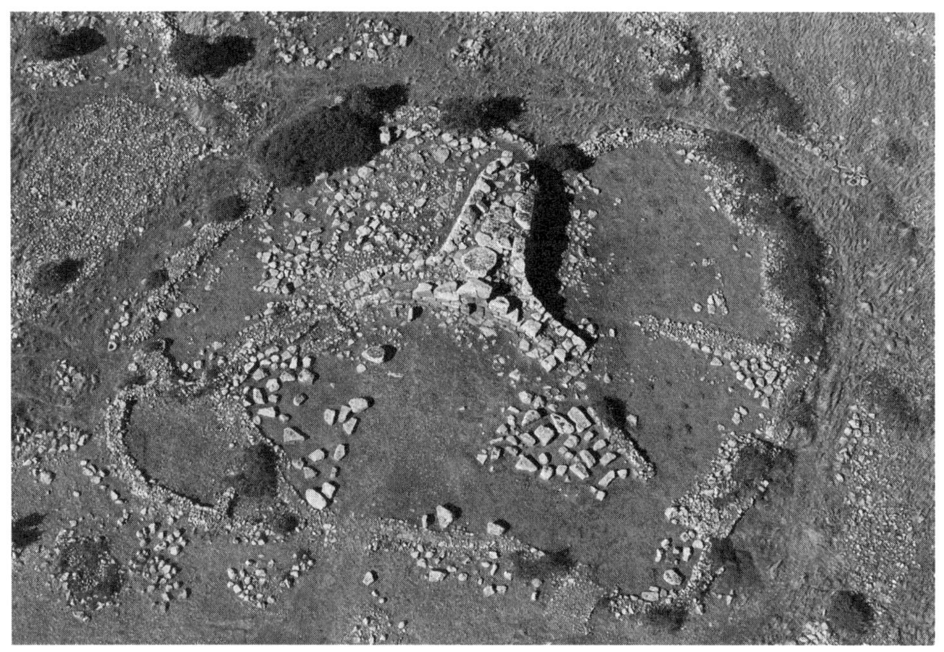

Fig. 3.4. Aerial view of the Siddi, Sardinia, Tombs of the Giants complex (photo by Francesco Cubeddu, 2011)

Fig. 3.5. A giant's tomb in Sardinia (photo by Gianni Careddu, 2015)

Fig. 3.6. Another giant's tomb at the Li Lolghi archaeological site near Arzachena, Sardinia, Italy (photo by Pjt56, 2010)

Investigative journalist Paola Harris interviewed Luigi Muscas on his property near Cagliari, Sardinia, during the fall of 2012. Harris writes:

> Luigi told me about the tombs and artifacts of giants (15 foot tall beings) who lived in Sardinia thousands of years ago. He told me that his father and his uncles, who also own land near his land, have dug up many bones and human artifacts. He also mentioned that traditional archeology does not accept this discovery and that his entire family has been threatened. He has been told over and over to keep this secret and not talk to the general public.[6]

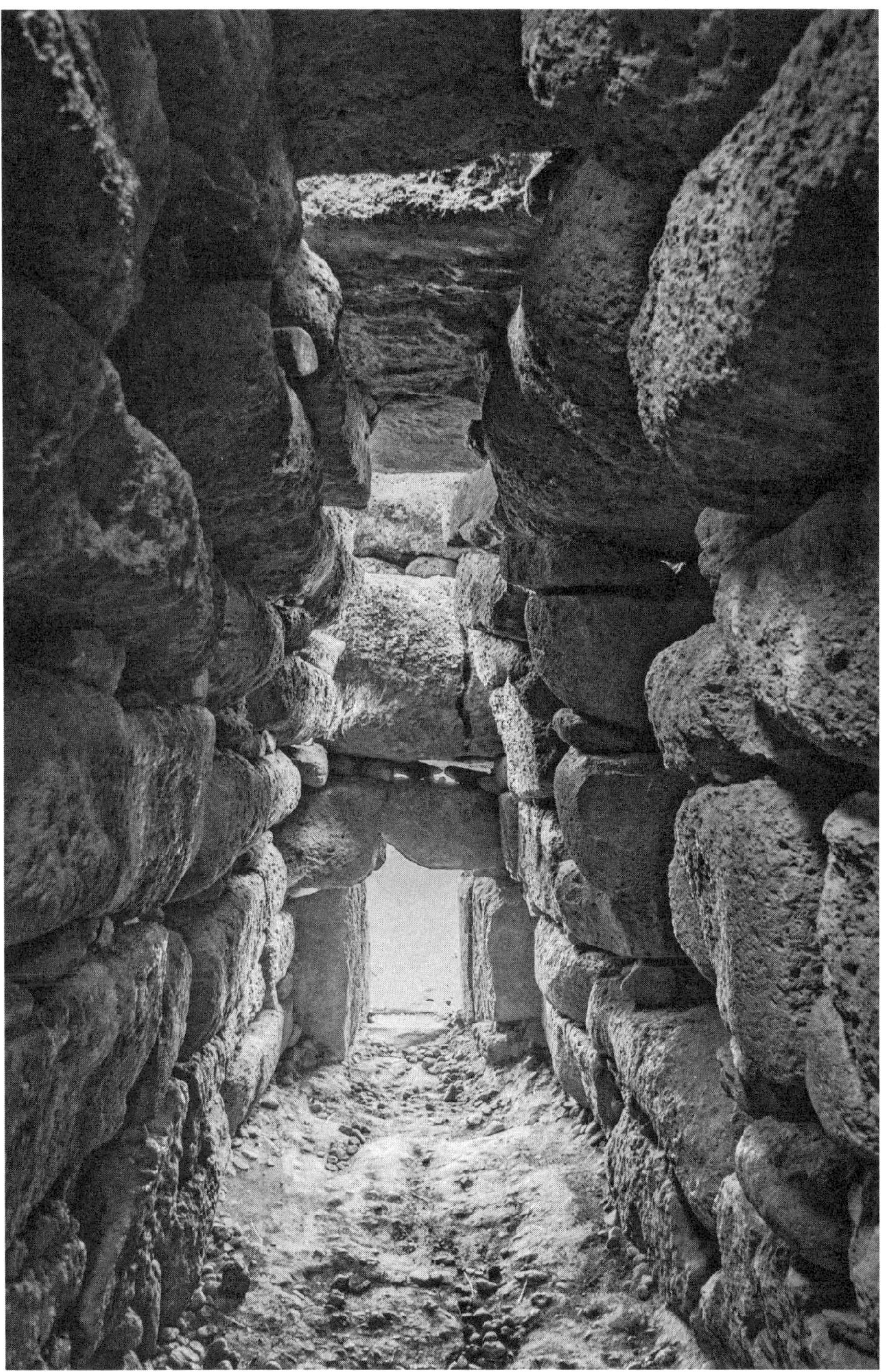

Fig. 3.7. Interior of the tomb of a giant in Cagliari
(photo by Fois Luigi, 2016)

Fig. 3.8. Tomb of a giant in Cagliari
(photo by Fois Luigi, 2016)

Fig. 3.9. Tomb of giants on the western slopes of the Sette Fratelli, in the municipality of Quartucciu, Sardinia (photo by Alex Follesa, 2012)

Caesar Augustus once recruited two towering ten-foot-tall giants, Posio and Secundilla, to lead the Roman armies into battle. After their victory the giants were celebrated as heroes, documented by Pliny. Because of their remarkable height they were preserved in the tombs of Sallust's Gardens. In 105 BCE, the Roman armies of Caepio and Manlius struggled mightily against a large tribe of roving German giants along the river Rhine. The bloodshed was brutal, leaving only twelve Roman soldiers who lived to tell the tale.

GERMANY: BAVARIAN CATACOMBS AND RHINELAND GIANTS

Giants are a common theme in the folklores and histories of Germany, too. The mystical realms of the Bavarian forests have spawned numerous tales of larger-than-life characters (see fig. 3.10). In the beer-guzzling town of Munich, workers unearthed forty well-preserved skeletons in a sand pit. The skeletons each averaged around seven feet in height and were accompanied with primitive stone tools.[7] This discovery in 1934 was soon forgotten as no other updates surfaced concerning the skeletons. Then in 1987 a pair of fishing teenagers discovered the femur joint of an apparent nine-footer resting at the bottom of the Rhine River. This area of Rhineland had been written about by Dutch scholar Dr. Jan Albert Bakker, in his book *Megalithic Research in the Netherlands, 1547–1911.* He described the giants of the Rhine as nearly naked wild men always carrying large clubs and eager to fornicate in public.

A Bavarian catacomb revealed thousands of giant bones arranged in a ritualistic method and buried under hundreds of normal-sized bones that had been set on fire at some point in the past. Known as the Breitenwinner Cave, news of the giant bones discovered there was first reported on by Berthold Buchner, the explorer who found them in 1535. Buchner, who was inspired by legends of a secret city of giants that lay beyond the massive underground catacombs as told by the citizens of Amberg, assembled a team and went to explore the catacombs. They eventually gained

Fig. 3.10. *Legends of the Rhine*, Helen Adeline Gruber (1929)

entrance and, throwing caution to the wind, began to explore the mysterious and darkened Breitenwinner Caves. Buchner writes:

> One of the leaders went in first, the other leader brought up the rear. We secured the entrance with rope and marked it with signs to avert danger, because if we should lose track of the ropes it would have been impossible for us to get out again. After fastening the ropes to a rock we descended 500 klafters [950 m] deep. Four honest strong men were selected to keep watch at the mouth of the mountain cave. Very soon we arrived at a very narrow cleft. One of our companions, a goldsmith, who at home had desired to be the first one in the cave, was so frightened by the sight of it that he deserted us notwithstanding his promise. But we crept on our stomachs some fifty Klafter [95 m] through this narrow cleft. There was a wider opening next to it but it did not stretch very far. First of all we came upon a wide space like a hall for dancing. When we crept in we found so many bones that the first of us had to pile them up in one place to make room for us to enter. The bones were very large as if from giants. We then reached a very narrow hole and had to squeeze through on our stomachs. At 200 Klafter [380 m] one comes into what seems like a beautiful spacious palace big enough to hold about 100 horses. It is lined at the top very handsomely with "grown" stones [speleothems]. There are eight or ten "grown" pillars and good seats at the sides. Here we found two skulls which to our surprise were enclosed by the rock, we could hardly hack them out with our tools. Each person took a piece, one the cranium, one the teeth, etc. There were many passages here and everywhere in the mountain; some of them we explored. All the caves and passages were full of big bones.[8]

In the 1970s two explorers relocated the cave, but said floods had made a mess of the place and there weren't any more giant bones lying around. And no mention of the giant dining hall carved elegantly within the walls of the mountain interior either.

About twenty elongated skulls were discovered in the Bavarian forests of southwest Germany in the 1980s. One of the elongated skulls is on display at the local museum in Tuchersfeld.[9] Armor belonging to a warrior at least eight feet tall can be seen in Reichsburg's castle.[10]

Ancient historian Strabo identified the German giants who lived east of the Rhine as being more wild, blonder, and taller than the giant tribes of Celtic warriors that inhabited northern Europe. These blond German giants were eventually eradicated just like their ancestors were.

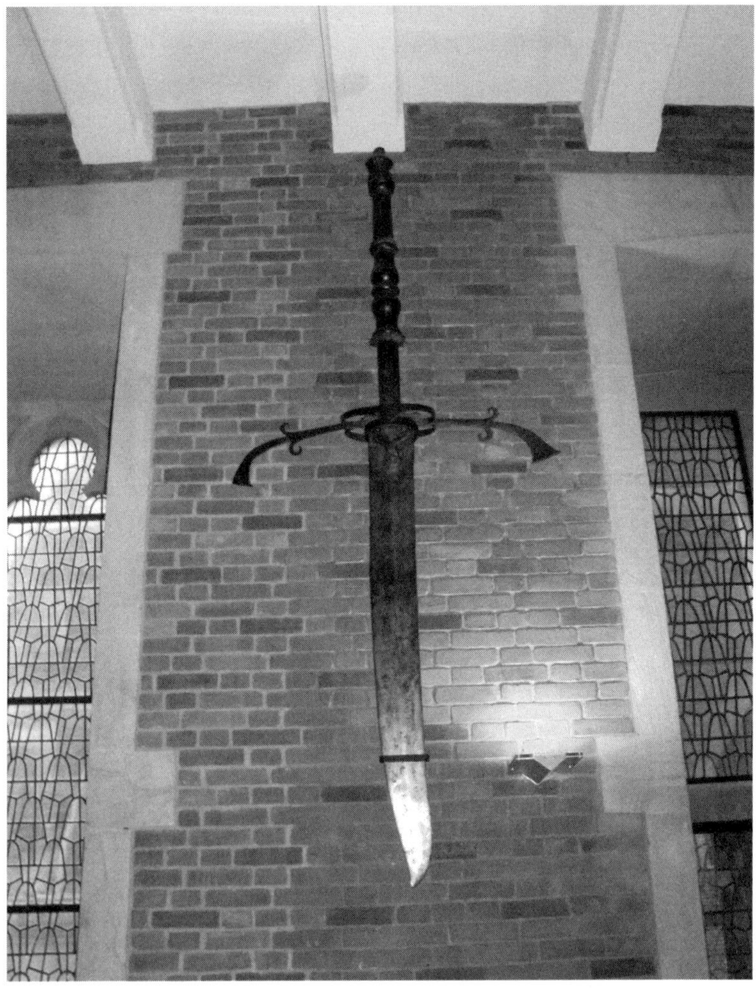

Fig. 3.11. A giant *zweihänder* (two-handed sword) in the historic town hall of Münster, North Rhine-Westphalia, Germany (photo by Anaconda74, 2013)

Fig. 3.12. *German Giant of the Rhine*,
Bethoven M. Tiano (2016)

Fig. 3.13. Celtic megalith in Germany, Saarland, near Scheiden (photo by Frabron, 2013)

But before these tall, wild, yellow-haired giants were destroyed, according to Strabo, they were declared to be the *Germani* to indicate that they were the authentic, the genuine, in a sense the original true giants. Their customs were much different from the Gauls and others who fought against them. Their whole life centered on hunting and military pursuits, and they showed little interest in religious matters or rituals.

The Romans fought against these fierce Germani giants for nearly three centuries. This experience taught the legionnaires to be an effective military force. Once they fought the Germani, they could not imagine anything worse.

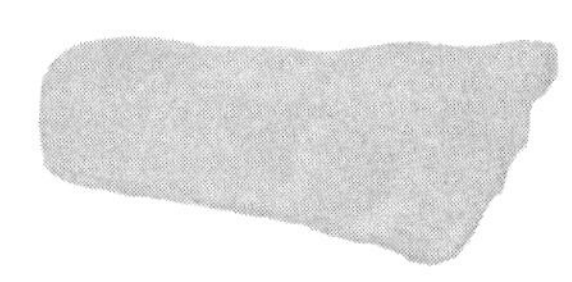

CHAPTER 4

Ancient Giants of Russia

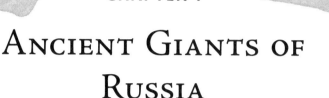

To have the truth in your possession you can be found guilty, sentenced to death.

Peter Tosh

The ancient giants of Russia aren't discussed much in the West, which has been blatantly anti-Russian for longer than most can even remember. But the Russian people and their culture are ancient. With new findings emerging through the frozen landscapes and a booming economy that's lifted most of its citizens out from underneath the communist rathole two decades ago, modern Russia has recently been eager to give up her secrets. An incredible discovery made there in 2014 threatens to overturn the conventional mainstream theories concerning the history of the planet. In the frozen tundra of southern Siberia, high on Mount Shoria, researchers found a series of megalithic stones that were assembled into a massive wall (see figs. 4.1–4.4). Some of these gigantic stones weigh over three thousand tons, boggling the mind when one thinks of how they could have been transported up the side of a rugged mountain and then stacked nearly fifty feet in the air. Some of the stones even appear to have been machine drilled and perhaps cut or sawed to reveal sharpened corners, flat smooth surfaces, and right angles.

These megalithic wonders of Russia easily blow away their closest competitors in the category of out-of-place mega stoneworks that can be found in the quarries of Cairo and at the ruins in Baalbek, Lebanon. These Russian megalithic stones are over twice as big; they also displayed a very unusual trait that caused the compasses of local researchers to malfunction. Archaeologist John Jensen first broke the story to Western audiences via his blog hosted by *Academia.edu:*

> The super megaliths were found and photographed for the first time by Georgy Sidorov on a recent expedition to the Southern Siberian mountains. The following images are from Valery Uvarov's Russian website. There are no measurements given, but from the scale depicted by the human figures, these megaliths are much larger (as much as 2 to 3 times larger) than the largest known megaliths in the world. (Example: The Pregnant Woman Stone of Baalbek, Lebanon weighs in at approximately 1,260 ton.) Some of these megaliths could easily weigh upward of 3,000 to 4,000 tons. There is little commentary on Valery's site, so the images are displayed here without much comment, other than my own limited observations.[1]

Another ancient site in Russia is Arkaim, also known as Russia's Stonehenge despite not having any gigantic stones standing guard over the area. The ancient site is best seen from the air, as it looks like whatever used to be there disappeared a long time ago. Like other ancient sites, Russia's Stonehenge is in perfect alignment to be used as a solar calendar with observations including sunsets and sunrises on the days of equinox and solstice, as well as sunsets and sunrises during low and high moon.

Adding more intrigue to this ancient and mysterious site was the discovery of an elongated skull in the vicinity.[2] Researcher Maria Makurova announced the discovery to the Russian news agency *TASS,*

Fig. 4.1. Megaliths of Russia
(photo by Василий Яр, 2014)

Fig. 4.2. Megalithic Russian wall
(photo by Василий Яр, 2014)

Fig. 4.3. Another view of the massive megalithic Russian wall (photo by Василий Яр, 2014)

Fig. 4.4. Panoramic view of the massive megalithic Russian wall (photo by Василий Яр, 2014)

explaining the elongated skull belonged to a female member of the indigenous Sarmati tribe who lived at the time in what is now central Russia. The ancient remains have left archaeologists too stunned to explain what an elongated skull is doing all the way in Chelyabinsk, a Russian city on the northeastern tip of the Ural Mountains. The typical answers were given of course to explain the elongated skull: the head-binding of a child's skull as per the tradition of the tribe. Never mind who these tribe members were trying to imitate in the first place.

The Sarmati tribes were Bronze Age warriors. It is claimed that they have left behind the various mounds that litter southern Russia. These mounds are called Kurgans and they share spooky similarities with other mounds found all over the world, including the mounds that once dominated the Midwest region of the United States of America. Some Kurgan mounds, estimated to be over two thousand five hundred years old, were recently excavated in Kazakhstan. They revealed the burial sites of several skeletons averaging more than seven feet in height.[3]

An eight-footer was dug up by researchers in the Aktobe region of Kazakhstan, and another eight-foot warrior was unearthed from an elaborate burial mound in Kumsai in 2014. That same year, more eight-foot giants were found in southern Russia near the Kuban River in modern-day Novopokrovskiy.[4] This small town near the border of Ukraine is mostly known for its sugar factories, so it was a big shock when local workers in charge of installing new high-voltage power lines unearthed a giant skeleton while digging a new foundation for their poles. Soon academic officials from the closest university showed up to inspect the findings and deemed them to be at least four thousand years old.[5] No word yet on where these giant skeletons may end up.

Although separated by thousands of miles and a massive ocean, both the mound-building cultures of the Ohio Valley and the Kurgan mound builders of the ancient steppes of Russia, Central Asia, and the Caucasus Mountains have exhibited skeletons and bones of giant proportions. Explorers of these mounds have unearthed the bones of men and women averaging from six and a half to eight and a half feet tall, all

Fig. 4.5. A Kurgan mound in Russia
(photo by Дар Ветер, 2013)

from an unknown culture anywhere from three thousand to five thousand years old or older. Nobody really knows.

In the 1920s explorers discovered a seven-foot giant skeleton in the Latoyust range of the Ural Mountains.[6] The two-thousand-year-old skeleton of a seven-foot-three-inches-tall woman warrior from Azerbaijan is on display at the Museum of History and Ethnography of Ganja, located in Ganja, Azerbaijan. Sadly there is no actual ganja or dreadlocked Rastafarians at this museum of Ganja located in the town of Ganja. But it does have the skeleton of a giant: a mighty woman warrior that might have once inspired the legends of the Amazonians. The placard on her display case reads, "*Kurgan. Woman funeral. The Bronze Age. 2000 B.C. The height of this woman buried in kurgan is 2m20sm.*

SKELETON OF PRE-HISTORIC GIANT FOUND

[By The United Press.]

Latoyust, Urals, Oct. 18.—The skeleton of a giant of the Ice Age, six feet eleven inches tall, was found in perfect condition here when excavators were digging a foundation for a theater. The skeleton of the prehistoric man is almost complete, according to sicentists who have examined it. They consider it of the highest scientific importance and it will be exhibited.

Fig. 4.6. "Skeleton of prehistoric giant found" in the Ural Mountains (*Southeast Missourian*, October 18, 1927)

Fig. 4.7. The skeleton of seven-foot-three-inches-tall woman from 2,000 BCE on display at the Museum of History and Ethnography of Ganja, Azerbaijan

Near there are personal plates and folding for hair."[7] Because even giant warrior women still took forever to do their hair before battle.

In Kazakhstan, researchers have been digging up seven- and eight-foot warrior skeletons in recent decades, usually found in ancient

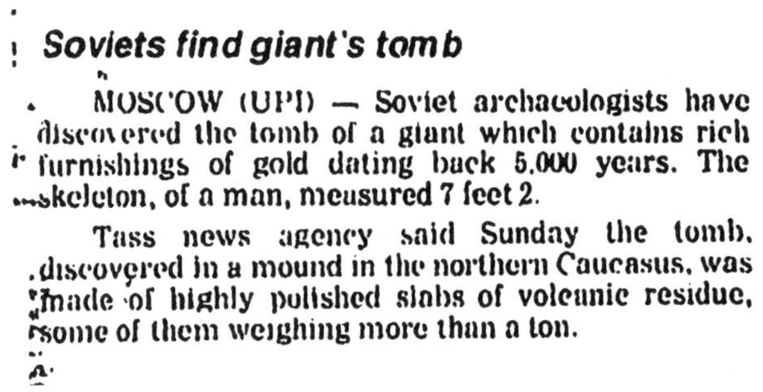

Soviets find giant's tomb

MOSCOW (UPI) — Soviet archaeologists have discovered the tomb of a giant which contains rich furnishings of gold dating back 5,000 years. The skeleton, of a man, measured 7 feet 2.

Tass news agency said Sunday the tomb, discovered in a mound in the northern Caucasus, was made of highly polished slabs of volcanic residue, some of them weighing more than a ton.

Fig. 4.8. "Soviets find giant's tomb"
(*Deseret News*, March 29, 1976)

burial mounds and Bronze Age stone vaults (see fig. 4.8).[8] Traces of the Kurgan genes can still be seen in the appearance of Nicolai Valuev, a modern-day giant and current Russian heavyweight champion. Valuev is a seven-foot-tall, three-hundred-pound boxer with unmistakable caveman Cro-Magnon cranial features. It wouldn't have been fun having to fight a whole tribe of his kind when you were at best five and a half feet tall.

Svyatogor was a warrior giant of Russian folklore, said to be a man so monstrous of size that when he walked, the top of his helmet swept away the clouds.[9]

In 1945, the *Washington Post* reported on a find by Soviet soldiers on a reconnaissance mission high in the Russian Himalayas:

Giant's Skeleton Found by Soviets

> The skeleton of a giant, with a skull 33 inches around and a shinbone 33 inches long, has been found in the Tien mountains of Russian central Asia north of the Himalayas, the Russian official agency, Tass, reported yesterday in a broadcast.[10]

A thirty-three-inch tibia bone indicates that this skeleton was indeed a real giant, measuring between eleven and twelve feet high. The *Lethbridge Herald* takes a closer look at the supposed twelve-foot-tall Soviet giant skeleton discovered in Russia:

Fig. 4.9. *Svyatogor,* Ivan Yakovlevich Bilibin
(Oil painting, 1900s, 2016)

> Discoveries made by scientists during World War II tend to show that this old earth on which we live hides many secrets in her breast. Among all the discoveries that are said to have been made by Russian scientists [this one] is the strangest and eeriest, says the Fort Williams Times-Journal. The report came from Russia and settlements between 25,000 and 100,000 years old had been revealed and a new island found in the Laptey Sea off Northern Siberia. Soviet scientists are said to have dug up fossil remains of a giant whose skull measured 33 inches in circumference and whose shin bone measures 33 inches long . . . he must have had a leg length not less than six feet. One can imagine the length of his stride as he moved about in a hurry. It long has been known that fossils indicate unanswerably that at one time animals and reptiles of enormous size lived on our earth. In such a period men, in order to survive at all, probably were much larger than modern man. Therefore the old legends of giants of the past well may have had a basis in truth.[11]

In 2004 Russian archaeologists discovered another elongated skull in Russia, this one found in the mountain regions of the northern Caucasus. It now resides at the Pyatigorsk museum of regional studies in the vacation-friendly city of Pyatigorsk located on the Podkumok River. *Pravda,* the Russian news agency, which sometimes reports news, first documented the elongated skull in 2005 after interviewing Vladimir Kuznetsov, doctor of historical sciences, an expert in the history of the North Caucasus. Kuznetsov says (translated into English):

> The skull is part of culture of the ancient Alani. Approximately, it dates back to the third to fifth centuries A.D. These strange skulls appeared at the same time when the Sarmatian and Alani hordes came around. Some of the nomads moved for the North Caucasus in the fifteenth century. Researchers have repeatedly proved that the skulls had been deformed on purpose; ropes or special blocks were tied tightly round the heads of infants, over the temples. The

> custom went out of fashion by the seventeenth century. The reason behind the deformation phenomenon is still unknown. It is hard to say whether the methods worked effectively or not since nobody ever conducted scientific experiments regarding the binding of the infants' heads.[12]

Sorry, but despite Kuznetsov's claims, not all elongated skulls have been proven to be from the results of child head-binding tactics. Why is it so hard for people to believe that a past race of giants, some even with elongated skulls, once lived on this four-billion-year-old planet that we call Earth? Why do we refuse to accept this greater ancestor into the ranks of once mighty human beings?

Armenia, a tiny nation near the border of Turkey and once part of the Soviet empire, has its fair share of giants inhabiting their ancient mythologies as well. In 2012 a Russian television crew assembled to film a documentary, *City of Giants,* about the giant eight-foot skeletons that had been unearthed by an archaeological team at the ancient complex of Goshavank.[13] The director of the historic site, Artsrun Hovsepian, explained that the giant bones had been found after digging for a new road in 1996. According to locals, giant bones have been found all throughout the region, including one skull that was so massive that it was double the size of a normal head. In Goris, a town less than five miles away, another giant eight-foot skeleton was discovered by a tractor driver digging a new foundation. This discovery made in 1984 was unique because the giant was still clutching his iron metal sword that was still rusting when it should have been completely crumbled to rusty dust.[14]

Pavel Avetisyan, director of the Russian Institute of Archaeology, claims that a recent discovery in Gyumri of a massive giant skeleton has challenged everything he's been taught to believe in according to the teachings of mainstream academia. Avetisyan says, "I was just taken aback, because, probably, the thumb of such a person would be thicker than my arm. I myself participated in the excavations and have often

Fig. 4.10. *The Terek Cossack host,* born near Voronezh, Russia, stood 2 m 40 cm, or about 8 feet tall! Timofei Bakulin, 1894–1936 (*Rephaim23,* 2015)

found the remains of people who were much taller than me . . . more than 2 meters."[15]

Remember that two meters is roughly eight feet tall, which is still kind of short compared to the giant warriors spoken of in Armenian history. Their warrior giants lived in the valleys near the river Vorotan in southeast Armenia. There in the mountain villages of Hot Springs, a great tomb was opened in 1966 that revealed a mass burial of giant skeletons. According to archaeologist Vazgen Gevorgyan, "The entire population of the village of Hot Springs says it found the skeletons of giants." In particular, Razmik Arakelyan personally saw the graves of two giants. He remarked that "all who saw were very surprised and felt that the place should be explored."[16] Gevorgyan did reconnoiter the area for more giant artifacts and found some in the neighboring village of Tandzatap where one tibia bone reached the waist of the town's tallest member.

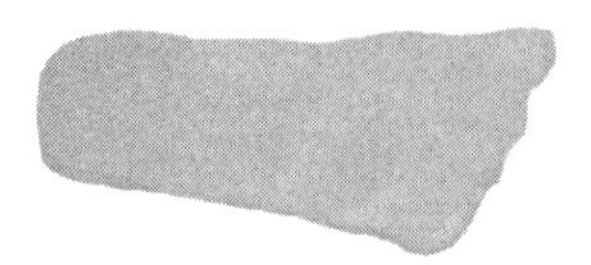

CHAPTER 5

Ancient Giants of Malta and Greece

It is the mark of an educated mind to be able to entertain a thought without accepting it.

Aristotle

MYSTERIOUS MEGALITHS ON MALTA, GOZO, AND COMINO ISLANDS

Three small islands in the Mediterranean Sea contain some of the biggest and most mysterious megalithic monuments in the world. The islands of Malta, Gozo, and Comino ominously float south of Sicily and to the east of the sprawling North African coastline. These tiny islands share a history of strange monuments, elongated skulls, and legends of giants that date back thousands of years. More than twenty Neolithic stone temples have been discovered on these islands, with mainstream estimates dating them around 4000 to 2500 BCE. All were built and lifted with ease, it seems, despite some stones weighing in excess of fifty tons each.

Malta, the biggest and most populated island of the three, is home to a series of awe-inspiring megalithic monument complexes known as

Tarxien, Hagar Qim, and Mnajdra. When early nineteenth-century explorers began excavating these megalithic sites they were under the impression that they had been erected by an extinct race of antediluvian giants. One of the earliest printed accounts of the Maltese Islands was published in 1536. It was written by the French academic Jean Quintin d'Autun, who made a convincing case, based on local folktales, that Malta had indeed been inhabited by giants in the days of yore.

The first excavations occurred at the Ġgantija "Giant's Place"[1] temple complex on the island of Gozo from 1816 to 1826. Now a UNESCO World Heritage Site, some of the stones at the Ġgantija complex are said to be among the largest freestanding stones in the world (see fig. 5.2).

The Tarxien temple complex in Malta is host to its own private springs and four megalithic structures that conjure up images of sword and sorcery movies (see figs. 5.3–5.6).

Fig. 5.1. An illustration of the Ġgantija megalithic temple in Gozo, Malta (from the series *L'Univers pittoresque*, Augustin François Lemaître, 2013)

Fig. 5.2. Megalithic temple, Ġgantija, at Gozo, Malta
(photo by Dietrich Michael Weidmann, 2012)

Fig. 5.3. Entrance into the megalithic Tarxien temples in Tarxien, Malta,
through the reconstructed trilithon doorway (photo by Thomas W. Fiege, 2016)

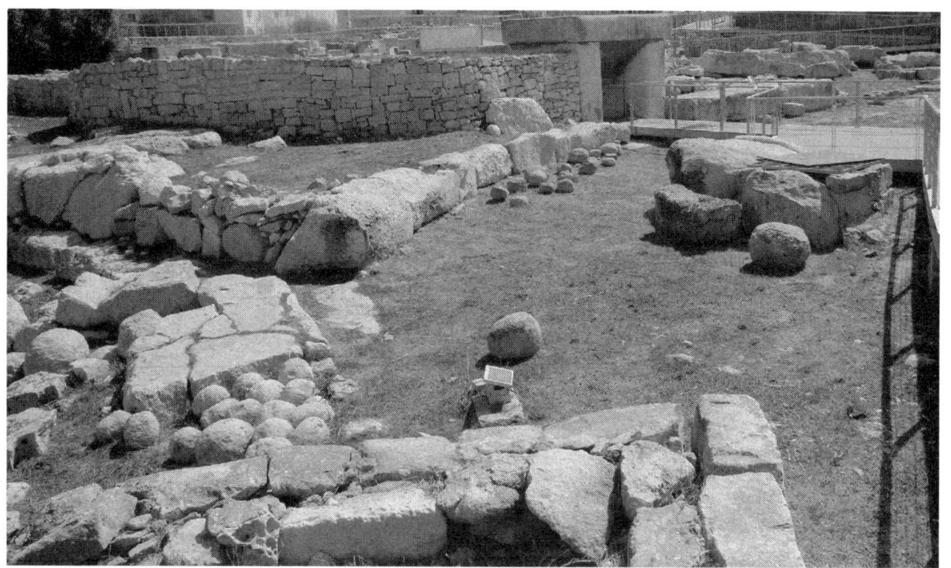

Fig. 5.4. Part of the excavation of the prehistoric Tarxien temples in the town Tarxien, Malta (photo by Karelj, 2014)

Fig. 5.5. Neolithic temple in Tarxien, Malta (photo by Bulbul, 2003)

Fig. 5.6. Entrance to the Tarxien temple in Malta (photo by Bulbul, 2003)

The Hypogeum, another mind-blowing megalithic site in Malta, is comprised of massive stoneworks arranged in a subterranean chamber. The Hypogeum, a Greek word meaning "underground," has been mystifying visitors since the dawn of Western civilization and may very well be the oldest prehistoric underground temple in the world. It was rediscovered in 1902 by construction workers who stumbled upon it after falling through a roof while demolishing a building. In what seemed to be an underground sanctuary, archaeologists began excavating, discovering three levels of underground stone structures. Pioneering Jesuit archaeologist Manuel Magri was in charge of the excavations but died mysteriously before the publication of the site's first excavation report in 1907.

According to the report, the ancient site was described as a massive catacomb with three intricate levels sculpted around two thousand tons of rock. The walls of the ancient site were ornamented with geometric figures such as spirals, spheres, and pentagons, alongside images of flowers and depictions of animals.

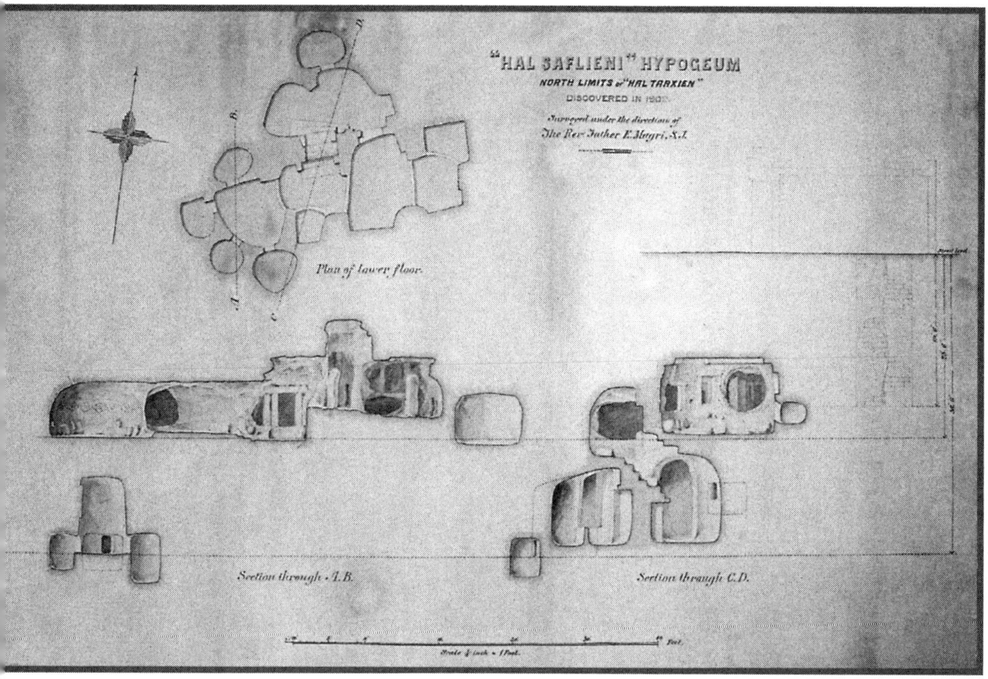

Fig. 5.7. Manwel Magri's architectural map of the Hypogeum in 1907

Fig. 5.8. The Hypogeum in 1924
(photo by Richard Ellis, 2008)

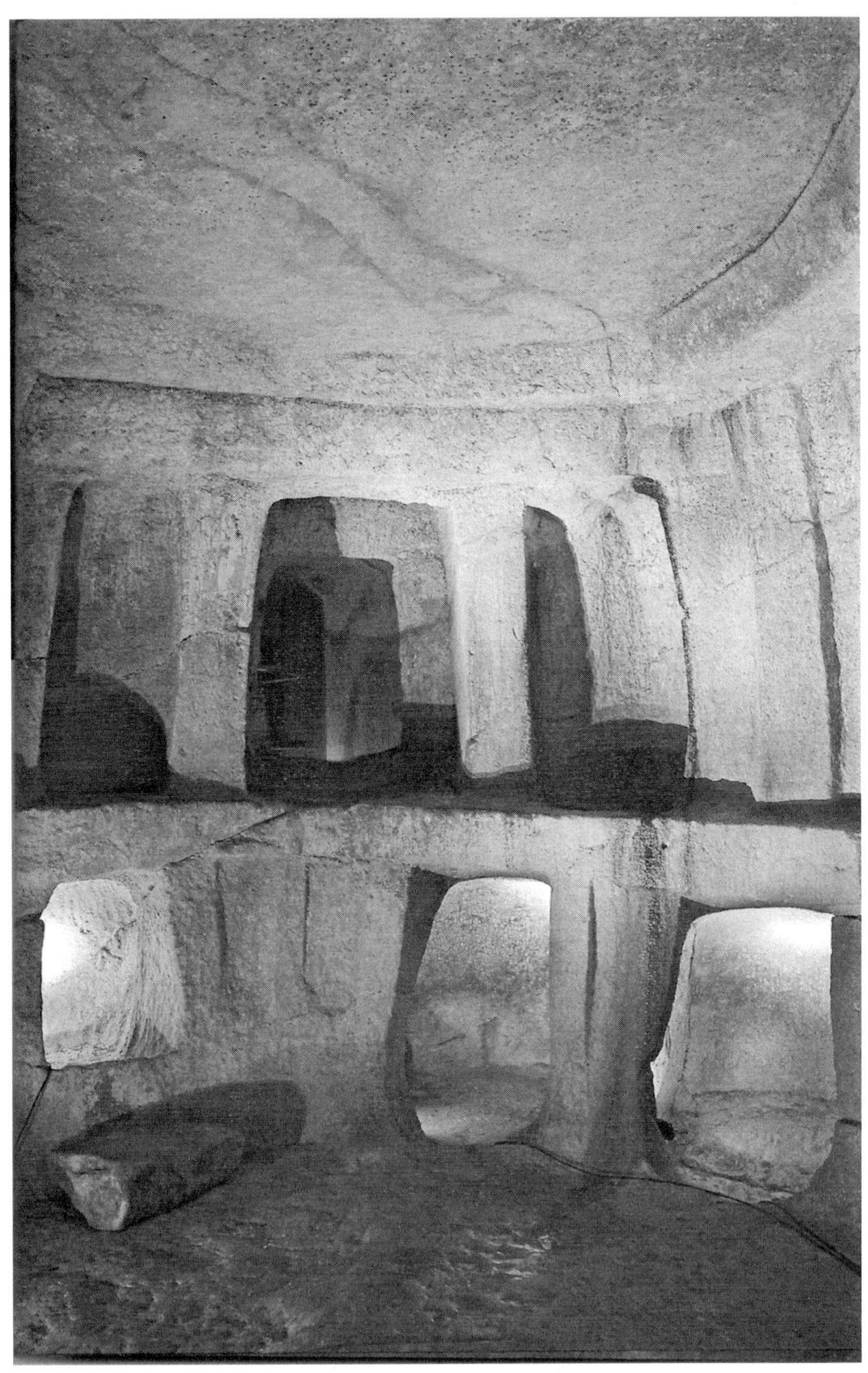

Fig. 5.9. The Hypogeum Chamber
(photo by A. Pace, 2004)

The Oracle room, one of the more enchanted rooms of the subterranean complex, was shown to exhibit different levels of acoustic properties that somehow reverberate all throughout the Hypogeum. It's like standing in a giant stone bell. Modern science has shown that the acoustic properties of reverberating sound can affect certain human emotions, and research done by Paolo Debertolis and Niccolo Bisconti of the Universities of Triest and Siena has proved that the Oracle room's construction was designed in a way to affect the emotions and psyche of the people who gathered there for spiritual and healing purposes.

In the acoustics of the Hypogeum we can find evidence of fractal nonlinear resonances, which is something that modern science has finally stumbled onto. Recent studies have shown that fractal nonlinear frequencies have the ability to physically alter matter.[2] How did this ancient race of giants know this? Did they use altered sound frequencies to levitate the massive blocks of megalithic stones? Was this how they flew them into place as some ancient legends have claimed?

Another mystery regarding the Malta megaliths are the numerous elongated skulls that have been discovered on the island, and the sudden disappearance of these skulls shortly after their discovery in the 1980s. More than seven thousand elongated skulls were found near the Hypogeum complex in a burial that baffled both the local historians and medical professionals alike. One of the skulls was even missing the fossa media joint that runs along the top of the skull head. Most of the skulls were displayed in the Archaeological Museum in Malta's capitol city of Valletta, until they all disappeared without a trace in the winter of 1985. None of the elongated skulls from Malta have been seen since. It's only thanks to the documenting and preserving of the skulls by Dr. Anton Mifsud and his colleague professor Charles Savona Ventura, Ph.D., who detailed the numerous strange characteristics like elongations, drilled and swollen occiputs, and weirdly developed temporal partitions, that we have any evidence of their existence in the first place.

The elongated skulls in Malta are unlike any known skulls currently found in the human race, although elongated skulls have also been discovered in Iran, Egypt, the Congo and the Sudan, Iraq, Syria, and also on the other side of the world in places such as Peru, Mexico, and Bolivia. *National Geographic Magazine* first wrote about these enigmatic Maltese skulls in the 1920s:

> From an examination of the skeletons of the polished-stone age, it appears that the early inhabitants of Malta were a race of long-skulled people of lower medium height, akin to the first people of Egypt, who spread westward along the north coast of Africa, whence some went to Malta and Sicily and others to Sardinia and Spain.[3]

Another Malta megalithic masterwork is the Hagar Qim, with massive stones joining together so effortlessly they can be compared with the seemingly fused blocks of the Valley Temple, next to the Sphinx at Giza and the walls of the Sacsayhuaman in Peru.

Fig. 5.10. A close-up of the tight stonework of Hagar Qim (photo by Kritzolina, 2014)

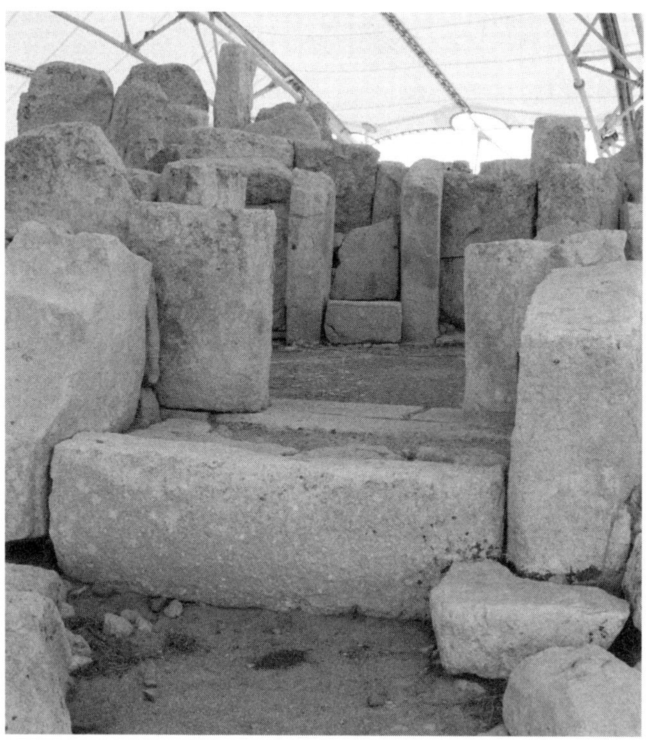

Fig. 5.11. Megalithic ruins of Hagar Qim
(photo by Kritzolina, 2014)

Stories of giants around these three islands aren't reserved to just ancient stones and folktales but are also told in modern times as well. According to Anton Mifsud, a prominent pediatrician from the island of Gozo, a giant skeleton was uncovered while workmen were digging a foundation for his expanded office building. The laborer who discovered the skeleton and Mr. Mifsud himself estimated its length being close to eight feet tall.[4] The bones were eventually seized by the local authorities, who promptly lost them, which is a good way to ensure no further scientific investigation on the supposed giant bones ever comes to light.

Another interesting fact about Malta is the extreme antiquity of the sites. Some ancient temples can be found submerged underwater, proving that these lands were subjected to the floods of the past, which is exactly the era when giants roamed the earth. Although mainstream academia denies the claims of submerged temples off the coast of Malta, in 1994 Commander S. A. Scicluna was quoted in the *Malta Sunday Times* as having discovered the temple complex one and a half miles from land, and at a depth of no more than twenty-five feet. Unfortunately the commander died mysteriously before meeting journalist Graham Hancock, who wished to verify the find, and the precise location of the site remains a mystery.

Nevertheless, it's been known since 1536 that an ancient megalithic structure once existed inside Valletta's Grand Harbor, at the foot of Fort Saint Angelo. Medieval mapmaker Jean Quintinus wrote that the temple extended over "a large part of the harbour, even far out into the sea."[5] And in 1606, Hieronymus Megeiser described the temple as being constructed of "rectangular blocks of unbelievable sizes."[6] In addition to the rising water levels, time also swallowed the civilization that erected these mighty megalithic monuments. As the temple complexes became forgotten, only the legends of giants remained.

But anti-giant skeptics, like "folk science"[7] historian Adrienne Mayor, think that the legends of giants come from the ancient discoveries of extinct mammoth and dinosaur bones. Much as we do today, the ancient Greeks and Romans collected and measured the petrified bones they found and proudly displayed them in temples and museums honoring the past. In her book *The First Fossil Hunters: Paleontology in Greek and Roman Times,* Mayor claims that the discovery of mysterious fossils helped support existing Greek myths and fueled the creation of fanciful new ones. Fossils found and displayed in antiquity on the island of Samos were nothing but mastodon bones even though they were believed by the ancient Greeks to be the genuine bones of their fifteen-foot-tall ancestral heroes.

This theory ignores the fact that the Greeks believed in ancient giants in the first place. Why would they need to make up a belief in ancient giants when confronted with strange gigantic bones? Why not assume these bones to just be the bones of extinct monsters? The fact that not only the ancient Greeks but pretty much every other culture on the planet shares the same beliefs about an ancient race of giants should be enough to convince anyone of their existence. Why instead choose to believe that giants and other so-called monsters were just figments of ancient creative minds that had nothing better to do than invent fantasies based on seeing mysterious and huge petrified bones? Kate A. Robson Brown, Ph.D., an anthropologist at the University of Bristol in England, thinks that some of Ms. Mayor's fossil-myth connections may be a stretch. As she noted in a recent issue of *Natural History* magazine, "Many cultures around the globe have colorful giant lore—Norse fables and Australian creation stories come to mind—without the benefit of rich fossil deposits."[8]

GREEK GIGANTES

The legends and myths of ancient Greece are steeped in giant folklore. Some of history's earliest writings are the tales of ancient giants. The Gigantes were an ancient Greek tribe of a hundred giants born from Gaia—the goddess of Earth. Legends say these giants rebelled against their masters but were all killed by the gods. The mighty Enceladus

Fig. 5.12. *Titans and Giants,* Gustave Doré (illustration for the 1890 printing of *Dante's Inferno*)

was defeated by Athena and buried beneath Mount Etna while Polybotes was crushed by a flying island hurled at him by Poseidon. The Greeks depicted the giants as primitive spear-chucking warriors dressed in animal skins, and Homer wrote that they were a gigantic and fierce race of men that were eventually exterminated by the gods. But Hesiod considered them divine beings, and later Greek poets immortalized them as Titans. An ancient verse from one of Ovid's poems even adds a reptilian twist:

> Titans, gave birth to the Gigantes, that is, monstrous and unconquerable giants, with fearful countenances and the tails of dragons.

Some of the names of the ancient Greek giants as listed in the *Dictionary of Greek and Roman Biography and Mythology:*

Agrios (Agrius): A Giant clubbed to death by the Moirai (Moirae, Fates) with maces of bronze.

Aigaion (Aegaeon): A Giant slain by Artemis with her arrows in the war against the gods.

Alkyoneus (Alcyoneus): King of the Giants who was slain by Hercules.

Aristaios (Aristaeus): The only Giant to survive the war against the gods.

Azeios (Azeus): A Giant who fought in the Titan Wars.

Hippolytos (Hippolytus): A Giant slain by an invisible cape-wearing Hermes.

Mimas: A Giant slain by Hephaistos and a cauldron of molten iron.

Porphyrion: King of the Giants who attempted to rape Hera but was double-teamed to death by the fistic fury of Zeus and Hercules.

In 8 BCE, ancient Greek historian Hesiod wrote about the origins and parentage of the giants:

> Then the son [Kronos (Cronus)] from his ambush stretched forth his left hand and in his right took the great long sickle with jagged teeth, and swiftly lopped off his own father's [Ouranos' (Uranus')] members and cast them away to fall behind him. And not vainly did they fall from his hand; for all the bloody drops that gushed forth Gaia (Gaea, the Earth) received, and as the seasons moved round she bare the strong Erinyes (Furies) and the great Gigantes (Giants) with gleaming armour.[9]

Around the same time, Homer was describing those lost ancient races in his epic poem the *Odyssey:*

> [King Alkinoos (Alcinous) of the Phaiekes (Phaeacians) addresses of his people:] "In the past they [the gods] have always appeared undisguised among us at our offering of noble hecatombs; they have feasted beside us, they have sat at the same table. And if one of us comes upon them as he travels alone, then too they have never as yet made concealment, because we are close of kin (egguthen) to themselves, just like those of the Kyklopes (Cyclopes) race or the savage people (phyla) of the Gigantes (Giants)."[10]

In his *Library of History* series Diodorus Siculus, the Sicilian Greek scholar of the first century BCE, writes:

> When the Gigantes (Giants) about Pallene chose to begin war against the immortals, Herakles fought on the side of the gods, and slaying many of the Sons of Ge (Gaea, the Earth) he received the highest approbation. For Zeus gave the name of Olympian only to

Fig. 5.13. *Odysseus in the Cave of Polyphemus*, Jacob Jordaens (early seventeenth century, oil on canvas, Pushkin museum)

> those gods who had fought by his side, in order that the courageous, by being adorned by so honourable a title, might be distinguished by this designation from the coward; and of those who were born of mortal women he considered only Dionysos and Herakles worthy of this name. Herakles then moved on from the Tiber [River of Rome], and as he passed down the coast of what now bears the name of Italia (Italy) he came to the Kumaion (Cumaean) Plain. Here, the myths relate, there were men of outstanding strength the fame of whom had gone abroad for lawlessness and they were called Gigantes. This plain was called Phlegraian (Fiery) from the mountain which of old spouted forth a huge fire. Now the Gigantes (Giants), according to the account, on learning that Herakles was at hand, gathered in full force and drew themselves up in battle-order against him. The struggle which took place was a wonderful one, in view both of the strength and courage of the Gigantes, but Herakles, they say, with the help of the gods who fought on his side, gained the upper hand in the battle, slew most of the Gigantes, and brought the land under cultivation.[11]

The ancient Greeks weren't the only ones having a problem eradicating the post-flood world of giants. The tales of the eradication of the ancient lineage of giants in the Holy Lands are some of the most famous ever told.

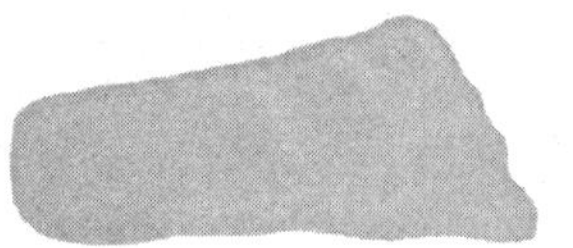

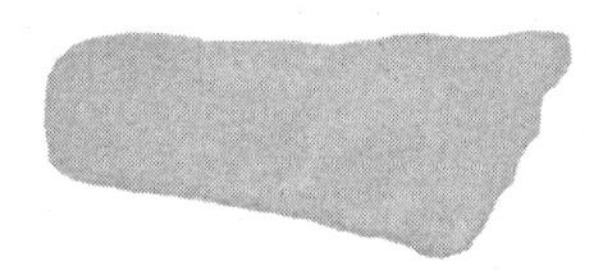

CHAPTER 6

Israel and the Ancient Biblical Giants

If history were taught in the form of stories, it would never be forgotten.

Rudyard Kipling

The Bible mentions thirty-six tribes of giants who fought for control over the Holy Lands in the days after the Great Flood. These giant tribes were the descendants of the Nephilim, a race of giants created by a race of fallen angels before the Great Flood. These angels, both the fallen and not fallen, were referred to in the ancient texts as the "Watchers" or the "Elohim." In an attempt to destroy the giants, the holy Elohim sent a flood to wipe them out and reset humanity. However, it didn't work and giants still roamed around the post-flooded world.

One of these giant tribes was the Amalekites, who originated from southern Arabia before migrating into modern-day Israel. Given their role in ancient history, it seems reasonable that the Amalekites had a pure strain of Nephilim DNA running through their giant veins. Numbers 13:28 verifies that the Amalekites were not only ancient but directly related to the Nephilim—the oldest race of giants who gave birth to the Anakims or the sons of Anak.

We even saw the descendants of Anak there.[1]

The thirty-six ancient tribes of Holy Land giants were:

Amalekites	Emims	Hittites	Manassites
Amorites	Emins	Hivites	Nephilim
Anakims	Eshkalonites	Horims	Perizzites
Ashdothites	Gazathites	Horites	Philistines
Avites	Geshurites	Jebusites	Rephaims
Aviums	Gibeonites	Kadmonites	Sidonians
Canaanites	Giblites	Kenites	Zamzummins
Caphtorims	Girgashites	Kenizzites	Zebusites
Ekronites	Gittites	Maachathites	Zuzims

Some of the biblical references to giants from the King James Version of the Bible:

> The Emims dwelt therein in times past, a people great, and many, and tall, as the Anakims. (Deuteronomy 2:10)
>
> Which also were accounted giants, as the Anakims; but the Moabites call them Emims. (Deuteronomy 2:11)
>
> That also was accounted a land of giants: giants dwelt therein in old time; and the Ammonites call them Zamzummins. (Deuteronomy 2:20)
>
> A people great, and many, and tall, as the Anakims; but the Lord destroyed them before them; and they succeeded them, and dwelt in their stead. (Deuteronomy 2:21)
>
> For only Og king of Bashan remained of the remnant of giants; behold, his bedstead was a bedstead of iron; is it not in Rabbath of the children of Ammon? nine cubits was the length thereof, and four cubits the breadth of it, after the cubit of a man. (Deuteronomy 3:11)

> And the rest of Gilead, and all Bashan, being the kingdom of Og, gave I unto the half tribe of Manasseh; all the region of Argob, with all Bashan, which was called the land of giants. (Deuteronomy 3:13)

> And these are the kings of the country which Joshua and the children of Israel smote on this side Jordan on the west, from Baal-gad in the valley of Lebanon even unto the mount Halak, that goeth up to Seir; which Joshua gave unto the tribes of Israel for a possession according to their divisions. (Joshua 12:7)

> And the coast of Og king of Bashan, which was of the remnant of the giants, that dwelt at Ashtaroth and at Edrei. (Joshua 12:4)

> All the kingdom of Og in Bashan, which reigned in Ashtaroth and in Edrei, who remained of the remnant of the giants: for these did Moses smite, and cast them out. (Joshua 13:12)

> And there was yet a battle in Gath, where was a man of great stature, that had on every hand six fingers, and on every foot six toes, four and twenty in number; and he also was born to the giant. (2 Samuel 21:20)

> And Ishbi-benob, which was of the sons of the giant, the weight of whose spear weighed three hundred shekels of brass in weight, he being girded with a new sword , thought to have slain David. (2 Samuel 21:16)

> These four were born to the giant in Gath, and fell by the hand of David, and by the hand of his servants. (2 Samuel 21:22)

In the late 1930s a collection of giant bones was discovered on Mount Carmel in Israel; later these giant bones disappeared and some newfound discoveries of Neanderthal bones wound up getting all the attention. The authorities didn't want to give credence to the fact that the bones could have belonged to the mysterious and giant Nephilim or any of their descendants.[2] Still, the Bible also mentions twenty-two individual giants by name.

Adonizedec	Jabin
Agag	Jobab
Ahima	Lahmi
Amalek	Nimrod
Arba	Og
Beelesath	Ogias
Gog and Magog	Perizzites
Gogmagog	Sheshai
Goliath	Sihon
Hoham	Sippai
Horam	Talmai

Most of the giants named were rulers and kings. Most of the population living in Canaan either belonged to a normal-sized tribe or a giant tribe, while the rest preferred to live wild in the woods. Perhaps the most famous ancient giant of the Bible was the legendary Goliath. First Samuel 17:4 reads, "A champion named Goliath, who was from Gath, came out of the Philistine camp. His height was six cubits and a span. He had a bronze helmet on his head and wore a coat of scale armor of bronze weighing five thousand shekels."[3]

According to today's math this would make Goliath twelve feet tall and buff enough to wear a 150-pound coat of bronze armor. It seems that the "return of giants" as prophesized in various Jewish teachings has indeed been becoming true lately as a series of "giant" discoveries made in Gath are proving that not all biblical stories are just myths. Rabbi Adam Eliyahu Berkowitz writes for *Breaking Israel News:*

> Archaeologists in Israel have uncovered what they believe to be the enormous gates of Gath, the city of Goliath. The story of Goliath the

> Giant (1 Samuel 17) is a Bible classic with a clear message for young and old. However, equally important and less studied, is the role of Goliath and the Philistines as the physical and ideological enemies of David and the Messianic dynasty. A Bar Ilan University team of archaeologists estimate that the remains of the ancient Philistine city date back to the 10th century BCE. Two inscriptions discovered at the site had names similar to Goliath, giving more weight to their theory. The modern site, known today as Tell es-Safi, has been occupied almost continuously for nearly 5,000 years and is the focus of continuous archaeological excavations since 1899. Until now, it was not known that its iron-age remains were so extensive.[4]

The lead excavation leader of the Gath project, Professor Aren Maeir, told *Live Science:*

> We knew that Philistine Gath in the tenth to ninth century (BCE) was a large city, perhaps the largest in the land at that time. These monumental fortifications stress how large and mighty this city was. Most scholars believe that Gath was besieged and laid to waste by Hazael, King of Aram Damascus, in 830 BCE. The newly discovered gate is being hailed as one of the largest of its kind ever found. The gate is part of enormous and extensive fortifications, indicating the importance of the city.[5]

Besides Goliath's giant gate, archaeologists also discovered the presence of ancient iron smelting and the markings of a catastrophic earthquake that once rocked the city around the eighth century BCE. Curiously enough this earthquake was mentioned in the book of Amos. However, there has been no discovery yet of either David's slingshot or Goliath's giant skull, which was carried to Jerusalem after David cut off the defeated giant's head.

After defeating the giant Goliath, David went on to defeat the

Fig. 6.1. Tel es-Safi (Gath), Israel
(photo by Bukvoed, 2016)

Fig. 6.2. Ancient wall of Tel es-Safi (Gath), Israel
(photo by Bukvoed, 2016)

remaining giants of the Philistines, four of which were defeated spectacularly as told in 2 Samuel 21:15–22:

> When the Philistines were at war again with Israel, David and his servants with him went down and fought against the Philistines; and

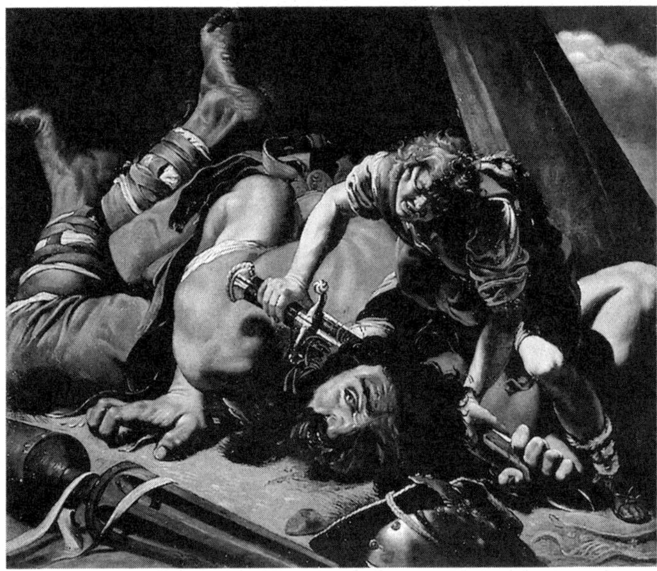

Fig. 6.3. *David Beheads Goliath,* Orazio Borgianni (oil on canvas, between 1609 and 1610)

David grew faint. Then Ishbi-Benob, who was one of the sons of the giant, the weight of whose bronze spear was three hundred shekels, who was bearing a new sword, thought he could kill David. But Abishai the son of Zeruiah came to his aid, and struck the Philistine and killed him. Then the men of David swore to him, saying, "You shall go out no more with us to battle, lest you quench the lamp of Israel." Now it happened afterward that there was again a battle with the Philistines at Gob. Then Sibbechai the Hushathite killed Saph who was one of the sons of the giant. Again there was war at Gob with the Philistines, where Elhanan the son of Jaare-Oregi the Bethlehemite killed the brother of Goliath the Gittite, the shaft of whose spear was like a weaver's beam. Yet again there was war at Gath, where there was a man of great stature, who had six fingers on each hand and six toes on each foot, twenty-four in number; and he also was born to the giant. So when he defied Israel, Jonathan the son of Shimea, David's brother, killed him. These four were born to the giant in Gath, and fell by the hand of David and by the hand of his servants.[6]

In his *Breaking Israel News* article, Rabbi Berkowitz further illustrated the post-flood world of the Holy Lands:

> Another source in the Babylonian Talmud relates that Sihon and Og, two kings mentioned later in the Bible, were descendants of the angel, Shamchazzi. The Midrash states that Og was alive in the time of Noah but escaped the flood by clinging to the side of the Ark. In Genesis 14:13, a "fugitive" (Palit) comes to tell Abram about Lot's capture. Og was named in Deuteronomy 3:11 as the only remaining man from the Rephaim, a biblical race of giants, and his bed was described as being enormous and made entirely of iron. The Nephilim are mentioned again in Numbers 13:33.[7]

The Bible relates that when Moses got close to Israel during his march out of Egypt, he sent a twelve-man reconnaissance party to spy on their future homeland. When the men returned, ten of them were so frightened they vowed never to enter Israel. According to Numbers 13:32–33:

> And they brought an evil report of the land which they had searched unto the children of Israel, saying, The land, through which we have gone to search it, is a land that eateth up the inhabitants thereof; and all the people that we saw in it are men of a great stature. And there we saw the giants, the sons of Anak, which come of the giants: and we were in our own sight as grasshoppers, and so we were in their sight.[8]

According to Rabbi Berkowitz, "Anak, translated as 'enormous,' was the archetypal giant and father of the race of men that lived in Hebron. The Midrashic sources explain that Anak was Og, one of the descendants of the Nephilim, and the fugitive from the flood. Another Midrash tells how Og attacked the Jews in the desert and Moses killed him."[9] When the giant king Og was laid to rest, the Bible mentions that his massive iron coffin was at least seventeen feet long. Og was apparently the last of the giant kings of the Bible, who were finally eradicated after Moses came to town.

In fact a good portion of the Bible is actually bashing the giants and claiming how wicked they were in the eyes of God the creator. Apparently the creation of the giants was one of God's biggest blunders of all time. On the shores of the Sea of Galilee lived the giants of the Emim and Zuzim tribes, who were eventually killed just like the Rephaim tribes of the nearby Ashteroth Karnaim.

There is even a Neolithic "wheel of giants" similar to the Stonehenge-type sites we discussed in Russia and Ireland. These megalithic ruins, known as Gilgal Refaim and located in the Golan Heights, were first discovered by Israeli soldiers during the war of 1967. They were rumored to be a burial site of the ancient giants, but recent archaeological examinations have yet to reveal any bones larger than usual.

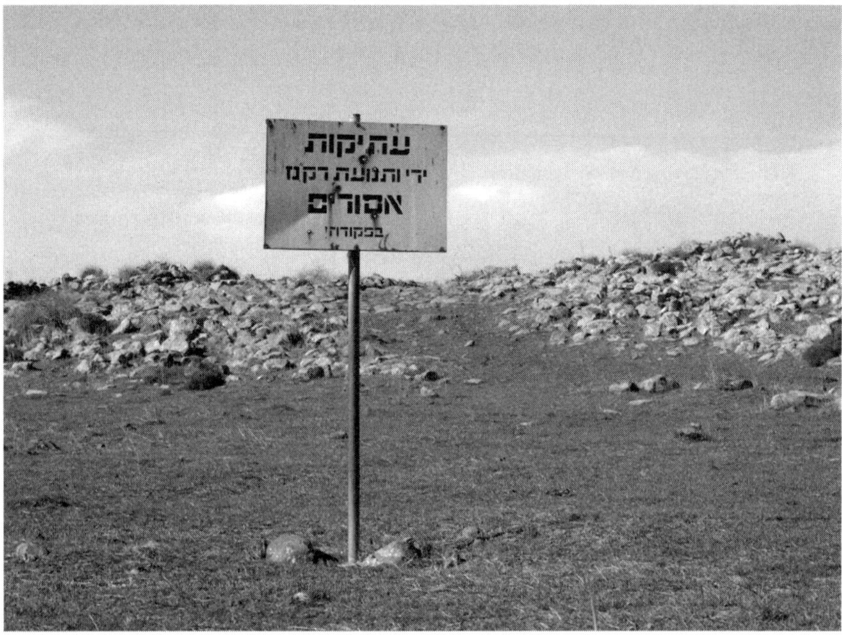

Fig. 6.4. Gilgal Refaim (wheel of giants), an ancient megalithic monument in the Golan Heights (photo by Staselnik, 2014)

Fig. 6.5. Exterior of Gilgal Refaim
(photo by Staselnik, 2014)

Fig. 6.6. Aerial view of Gilgal Refaim
(photo by אסף.צ, 2007)

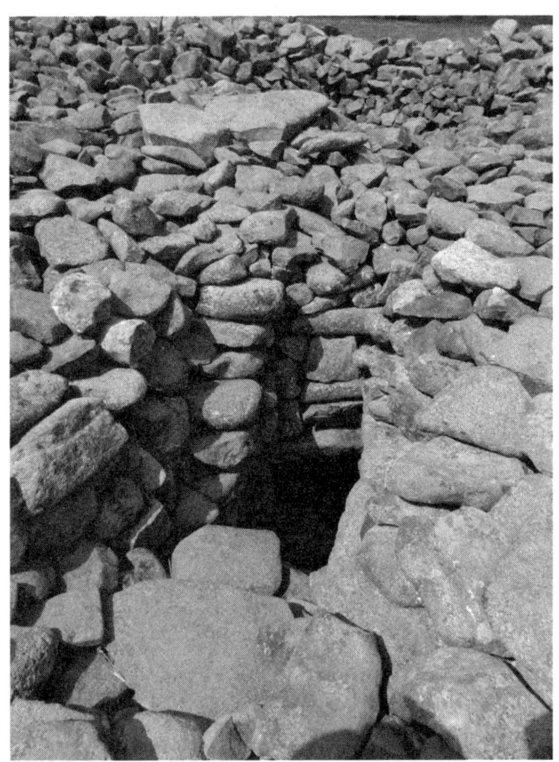

Fig. 6.7. Entrance to the Gilgal Refaim burial chamber (photo by Ani Nimi, 2011)

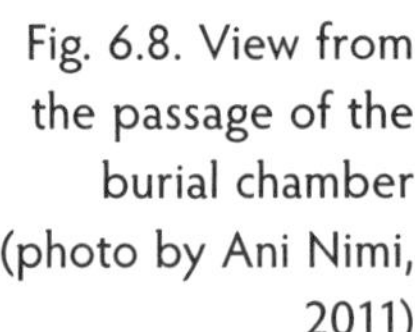

Fig. 6.8. View from the passage of the burial chamber (photo by Ani Nimi, 2011)

The plant, insect, dinosaur, and fossil records of pre-flood eras reveal huge growth cycles and long life spans. But what about humans? We know they lived for a long period of time. For example, Adam lived for 930 years and, according to the Islamic *Hadiths,* was even ninety feet tall! According to the book of Genesis the original patriarchs of Earth all had impressive life spans with some lives, like Methuselah's, approaching a thousand years. Noah lived to be 950 years old and was also a giant. Ron Wyatt, the controversial Australian archaeologist, on one of his first journeys to the believed site of Noah's Ark, high in the Turkish mountains, revealed the house of Noah and the grave of his wife, in which, he claimed, the coffin was eighteen feet tall. The military has secured the alleged site and dismissed Wyatt's claims.

First Chronicles 11:23 mentions that Beniah, a hero of David's army, slew an Egyptian giant who was more than eight and a half feet tall. The giants mentioned in the Bible were looked upon as being real historical persons and residents in the modern territories of Israel, Jordan, Lebanon, Syria, and Egypt. These mystical Middle Eastern lands are rich with traditions of giants and giant discoveries.

CHAPTER 7

Ancient Giants of Egypt, Syria, Iraq, and Iran

History is a wheel, for the nature of man is fundamentally unchanging. What has happened before will perforce happen again.

George R. R. Martin

DARIUS THE GREAT AND IRAN'S ANCIENT PERSIAN EMPIRE

Darius the Great ruled the Persian Empire at its zenith, leaving behind a legacy of goodwill and total militaristic domination. The Behistun Inscription, a multilingual engraving written on a mountain high in western Iran, was crucial to the decipherment of cuneiform script. It also depicts Darius as a giant standing tall over his minuscule captives. With a proclaimed lineage to the semi-divine rulers of Persia's bejeweled past, it makes sense that Darius was indeed a giant. When Alexander the Great conquered Persepolis in 330 BCE and sat upon the throne of Darius, his feet dangled in the air far from the quartz floor beneath

Fig. 7.1. The Behistun Inscription
(*L'Homme et la terre*, tome 1, 1905)

him. The tomb of Darius is a popular tourist attraction when visiting the ancient site of Persepolis, yet nobody knows for sure that it ever really held or holds the giant skeleton of Darius the Great. It would be interesting to excavate whatever is inside the tomb, and if it's a giant skeleton it might be worth the desecration.

IRAQ AND THE LEGEND OF GILGAMESH

In the nearby city of Kalar, in Iraq, the bones of men more than ten feet tall were discovered by archaeologists in the hills of Rahim in Rizgari city. Mohamed Ali, the official media mouthpiece of the Department of Archaeology, explained, "We found a number of graves here. The skeleton of the men are so big and tall that they are abnormal. These remains could date back thousands of years BC. We are now working on cleaning the graves. There are four of them. The height of men according to their skeletons is about 3 meters (about 10 feet) they are fascinating."[1] No other information has emerged about this discovery due to the secluded culture of Iran and the ongoing general destruction of Iraq.

The legendary giant Gilgamesh was the first hero of the ancient world. He was the historical ruler and builder of the city of Uruk nearly five thousand years ago. The poem that describes his tales, *The Epic of Gilgamesh,* is the oldest known piece of epic poetry ever written. It even has a flood myth almost identical to the one found in the Bible thousands of years later. Like Hercules, Gilgamesh was such a mythical figure that the idea of locating his tomb seemed unrealistic and a fantasy until 2003 when a group of German archaeologists shocked the world by announcing they had discovered his ancient lost tomb near a dried-up area of the Euphrates River in northern Iraq. Unfortunately, and not surprisingly, the Iraq war broke out shortly after and any updates of the discovery were never announced again. From the original *BBC* article in 2003:

> The Epic Of Gilgamesh—written by a Middle Eastern scholar 2,500 years before the birth of Christ—commemorated the life of the ruler of the city of Uruk, from which Iraq gets its name. Now, a German-led expedition has discovered what is thought to be the entire city of Uruk—including, where the Euphrates once flowed, the last resting place of its famous King. "I don't want to say definitely it was the grave of King Gilgamesh, but it looks very similar to that described in the epic," Jorg Fassbinder, of the Bavarian department of Historical Monuments in Munich, told the BBC World Service's Science in Action programme. In the book—actually a set of inscribed clay tablets—Gilgamesh was described as having been buried under the Euphrates, in a tomb apparently constructed when the waters of the ancient river parted following his death. "We found just outside the city an area in the middle of the former Euphrates River. The remains of such a building which could be interpreted as a burial," Mr. Fassbinder said. He said the amazing

> discovery of the ancient city under the Iraqi desert had been made possible by modern technology. "By differences in magnetisation in the soil, you can look into the ground," Mr Fassbinder added. "The difference between mudbricks and sediments in the Euphrates River gives a very detailed structure." This creates a magnetogram, which is then digitally mapped, effectively giving a town plan of Uruk. "The most surprising thing was that we found structures already described by Gilgamesh," Mr Fassbinder stated. "We covered more than 100 hectares. We have found garden structures and field structures as described in the epic, and we found Babylonian houses." But he said the most astonishing find was an incredibly sophisticated system of canals. "Very clearly, we can see in the canals some structures showing that flooding destroyed some houses, which means it was a highly developed system. [It was] like Venice in the desert."[2]

Gilgamesh was an interesting figure, and the discovery of his body would be a huge deal. The *Book of Giants,* recovered from the Dead Sea scrolls,* mentions the king Gilgamesh as one of the mighty antediluvian Nephilim giants who ruled before the flood. He was said to have been half-god, and somewhere between sixteen to eighteen feet tall! If this was confirmed it would turn the established timeline of history upside down and cause earthquakes throughout the halls of the academic world. No wonder they weren't in a hurry to dig him up.

EGYPT'S GIANT PHARAOHS AND MUMMIES

The ancient lands of Egypt are flush with mysterious monuments and tales of giants. You can even see them in the hieroglyphs upon the murals of wall paintings that dominate ancient temples. The depictions of some of the pharaohs clearly show a staggering height difference that cannot

*An article on the recovery of the text of the *Book of Giants* and its translations, by W. B. Henning, is reproduced in the appendix of this book.

be explained away as simply artistic license. In 2001 a skeleton known as the Giza Mulhern giant was dug up from a Fifth Dynasty mastaba tomb in cemetery 2500 in western Giza by archaeologists from Howard University. Despite the skeleton only measuring around six and a half feet, the skull and the jawbone were abnormally large, so much so that mainstream academia declared the Mulhern giant the first case of gigantism in ancient Egypt.[3] Yet, despite this first, the skull has been hidden away by academia and the remaining bones promptly lost.

Fig. 7.2. *Giant pharaoh*, Bethoven M. Tiano (2016)

Swiss nightclub mogul Gregory Spörri spent 1988 roaming around Egypt in search of mysteries in both inner and outer spaces and what he found ended up changing his life forever. About an hour's drive northeast of Cairo, Spörri met a family of ancient grave robbers in a farmhouse in Bir Hooker, where he was shown a mummified giant's finger that was wrapped in old rags and leather skin. An astonished Spörri told the prominent German newspaper *BILD.de,* "It was an oblong package, smelled musty. I was absolutely flabbergasted when I saw the dark brown relic."[4] Spörri was allowed to handle the giant finger and also photograph it next to an Egyptian monetary note to get a size comparison. He tried to buy the relic but the family refused to sell it, and Spörri returned to Switzerland armed only with a few photographs of the finger and a mind-blowing personal experience. The few scientists that he showed the photographs to all mocked him and didn't take him seriously, so Spörri put the photos away and continued to live his club-owning playboy lifestyle. But the thought of ancient giants once existing in Egypt kept nagging him. Twenty years after his first encounter with the giant finger, he returned to Egypt in hopes of rediscovering the mysterious relic of Bir Hooker. But the family of grave robbers and the finger had vanished.

GIANT FOOTPRINTS AND GRAVES IN SYRIA

At the ancient temple of Ain Dara in Syria, several huge three-foot-long footprints are clearly visible in the courtyard leading into the sanctuary of the temple (see fig. 7.3). The giant who made these impressions must have been fifteen to twenty feet tall!

In 2005, a group of Russian scientists led by Professor Ernst Muldashev announced they had discovered a grave of giants near the site of the giant's footprints at Ain Dara and also discovered more giant burial sites throughout Syria but were unable to excavate them due to various reasons, ranging from political to ideological. In a Q & A interview with *Pravda* Professor Ernst Muldashev explained:

Fig. 7.3. Giant footprints of Ain Dara
(Institute for the Study of the Ancient World Contact, 2016)

Q: Many a legend and fairy tale mention giants and titans. Why do you think no giant bones have been found so far?

A: Ancient giants may have never buried their dead in the ground the way we do. Different people in the present-day world bury the dead differently. It is a custom in India to burn the dead and throw the ashes in water. It seems to me that ancient people put the dead bodies into sarcophaguses where the bodies dematerialized and turned into a kind of energy blobs that were used by living people for various purposes. That is why the bones of giant people may never be found.

Q: Did you find any?

A: No, we did not. But we found the graves of ancient giants.

Q: Could you please elaborate.

A: The grave of Abel, the second son of Adam and Eve, is the most famous and significant grave. It is located in the vicinity of Damascus. . . . The tombstone of Abel's grave is a granite structure about six meters [nineteen and a half feet] long and 1.80 meters wide. There are orifices on the side of the gravestone. You can smell a strange odor if you get closer to the orifices.

Q: Has anybody ever tried to open the grave and study the contents?

A: Muslims will never allow anybody to open the grave. It would be regarded as desecration of a grave.

Q: You mentioned a few graves of the giants found by your expedition, did you not?

A: Yes, I did. The long search finally resulted in the discovery of several gigantic graves located near the city of Aleppo in Syria. The graves used to be a sacred place for worshippers. However, some locals told us that radical Muslims destroyed the cemetery a few years ago.

Fig. 7.4. Giant tomb of Abel located at the Nabi Habeel Mosque in Syria (photo by Toushiro, 2004)

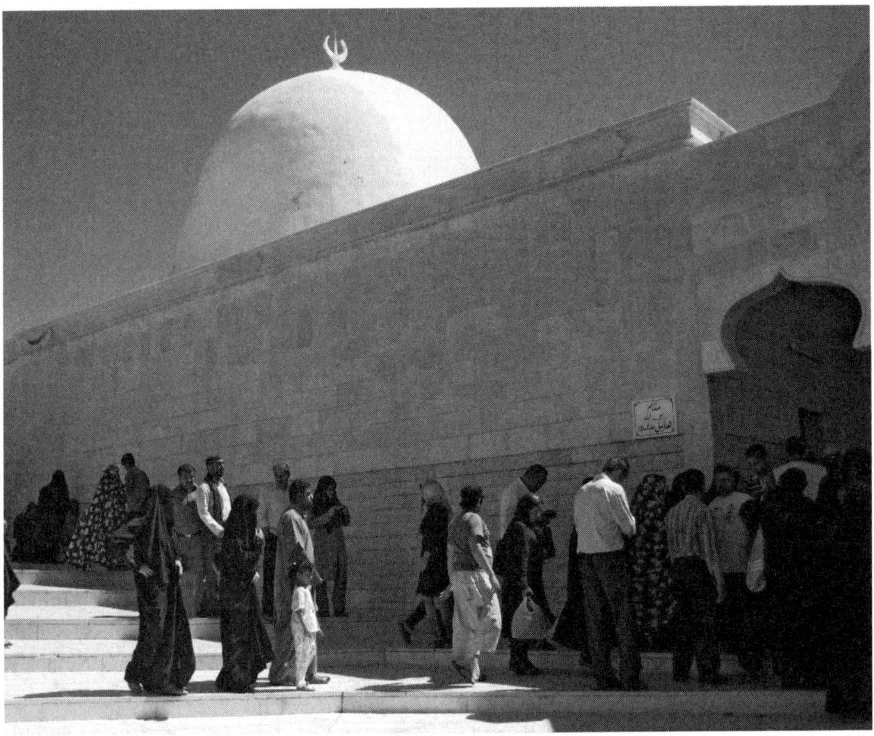

Fig. 7.5. Entrance to the Nabi Habeel Mosque to see the giant tomb of Abel (photo by Toushiro, 2004)

They bulldozed the tombstones. We could have started an excavation on the site but we never did. We did not know how the locals would react to our digging in their ground. The locals showed us another grave of a giant. It sits on top of the hill some 20 kilometers away from the destroyed cemetery. The locals call the place a "grave of a 7.5-meter man." The giant was called "Muhammad Attaul" or Muhammad the Tall One. Legend has it that the giant came down from Yemen. He was a miracle man, he could speak a form of Arabic used by the prophet Muhammad. He was killed and buried there. The treasure diggers vandalized the grave two years ago. They were caught and thrown into jail. Local peasants are now trying to restore the grave. They already placed a few boulders around it and built a stone fence.

Q: Do you really believe that giant people were buried in those graves?

A: Nobody can tell for sure until the graves are opened and bones are found. But the Syrian authorities are unlikely to authorize the opening of the graves.[5]

The Ras Shamra Tablets, discovered in 1928 in a mound near the ancient city of Ugarit, located on the Syrian coast, provide more information about ancient giants and frequently mention the Rephaim of Hebrew legend. The tablets even describe the Mesopotamian hero Gilgamesh as being sixteen and a half feet tall. The linguists who deciphered the cuneiform texts concluded they were written around the time of Joshua. According to pioneering Egyptologist Henry Hall, Ph.D., the Rephaim (giants) were the ones responsible for building all the megalithic monuments, dolmens, and the menhirs of Moab in eastern Syria. Considering that Syria has been and is currently being torn to shreds by imperialistic globalist forces, it's doubtful that any progress of digging up the bones of ancient giants will be happening there. Also there's little chance of excavating any time soon in either Iraq or Iran. Egypt is still moderately accessible, but the general uncertainty of the Middle East and the fear of radical Islamic terrorists have put a halt to most archaeological excavations.

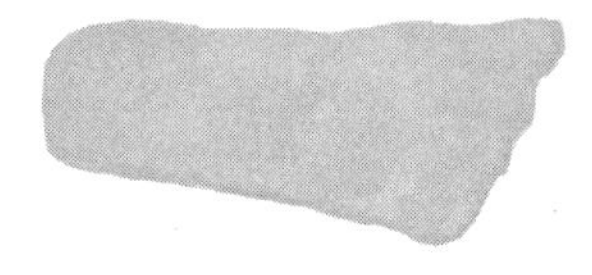

CHAPTER 8

Ancient Giants of Africa

I don't tell lies against anybody. That's why I always win all my wars.

Fela Kuti

The Nomoli figures of Sierra Leone, West Africa, were discovered by European missionaries in 1852 after they had come across an abandoned village. These mysterious carved soapstone figures date as far back as 17,000 BCE and prove the existence of an advanced ancient civilization prior to those in current West Africa. One of the figures clearly represents the head of a reptilian being that is holding some kind of basket in his hands. And the giants are represented as well in one of the figures that showcases a large human riding on a full-grown elephant. The local African tribes where the figures were discovered have long oral traditions and ancient memories of the giants who once lived there. African legends describe these powerful beings as courageous and very strong men with shining eyes and with voices that could be heard from one town to another. A legend tells that

> they wandered without let or hindrance to places where no man had ever been before. One could not look them in the face because their eyes were so bright that it hurt one's own eyes to look at them. It was like looking at the sun.[1]

An interesting discovery was made when a small metal ball was found in a hollow space inside a Nomoli figurine. Analysis by the Museum of Natural History in Vienna, Austria, revealed that it is made from chrome and steel. But the earliest-known production of steel is a piece of ironware unearthed in Anatolia (Kaman-Kalehoyuk) about four thousand years ago. How is this possible? This giant civilization was highly advanced and equipped with the right tools for modeling perfectly spherical objects like those found inside the figures. Other African legends talk about heavenly creatures banned from the divine empire and sent to Earth, similar to the "fallen angels" mentioned by various cultures.

A perfectly formed giant's footprint imprinted in granite was discovered in 1912 by a farmer called Stoffel Coetzee while hunting in what was called the Eastern Transvaal, South Africa. The four-foot-long footprint can be found in an outcrop of the Mpuluzi batholith, dated to around 3.1 billion years old. The giant that it belonged to would have been anywhere between twenty-three and twenty-five feet tall!

In 1936 two French archaeologists, Lebeuf and Griaule, led an expedition to Chad in North Central Africa. As they crossed the plains, they saw some areas covered with small mounds. Deciding to investigate, they dug up several egg-shaped funeral jars that contained the remains of a gigantic race, along with pieces of their jewelry and works of art.

> These giants, according to the natives, were called the Saos. Scholars who traced their history say they came from Kheiber, located north of Mecca, to Bilma, which is situated about three hundred miles

north of Lake Chad. A people with a "well-developed religion and culture," they grew in numbers and founded communities at Fort Lamy, Mahaya, Midigue, and Goulfeil. They lived in peace in their new land until the close of the ninth century when the Moslems made wars against them, intending to force their acceptance of the Islamic faith. The Saos giants who converted to the faith lived to become servants of the Arabs. But those who steadfastly refused to convert were eventually wiped out. By the end of the sixteenth century not many Saos remained.[2]

In *Timeless Earth,* author Peter Kolosimo writes about the giant ax handles discovered by the French captain Lafanechere at Agadir in Morocco.

> Discovered a complete arsenal of hunting weapons including five hundred double-edged axes weighing seventeen and a half pounds, i.e. twenty times as heavy as would be convenient for modern man. Apart from the question of weight, to handle the axe at all one would need to have hands of a size appropriate to a giant with a stature of at least 13 feet.[3]

Africa's Watusi warriors are famous for their elaborate dances and great height. Globetrotting writer and historian Glenn D. Kittler describes the Watusi in his children's book *Let's Travel in the Congo:*

> For the most colorful and exciting dancing, you must go to Ruanda-Urundi . . . east of the Congo. Here the ruling tribe is the Watusi, the tallest people in the world. It has been said that these giants are born six feet tall, and when you walk among them you can believe it. Men towering seven or eight feet are a common sight.[4]

Anthropologists can't account for the excessive tallness of the Watusi. They are at a loss for words, just as Marco Polo was before writing about his meeting with the giants of Zanzibar in his famous journals. Marco Polo writes:

> Zanzibar is situated off the coast of Tanganyika. Nearly 53 miles long and 24 miles wide, it is the largest coral island on the African coast. . . . Numerous bays, reefs, and islets are found along the western coast, while the eastern side is much more regular. Zanzibar is a very large and important island. It has a 2,000-mile coastline. All the people are idolaters, they have a king and a language of their own and pay tribute to no one. The men are large and fat, although they are not tall in proportion to their bulk. They are strong limbed and as hefty as giants. They are so strong that they can carry as many as four ordinary men. This is not altogether surprising because while they can carry as many as four men, they eat enough for five.[5]

Liongo was the mythical giant hero of the Swahili and Pokomo peoples of eastern Kenya (see fig. 8.1). Historians believe Liongo lived on the Kenyan coast as early as 1200 CE. A large section of Swahili poetry is inspired and dedicated to Liongo, including many popular wedding songs that are still performed today. Liongo would eventually become King of Ozi until the region's first Islamic ruler, Sultan Ahmad, had him chained and imprisoned. But the giant Liongo escaped to the mainland, where he lived with the forest-dwelling Watwa, spending his time perfecting his archery techniques and preparing to fight off the Muslim invaders, unaware that his own son would be the one to deliver the fatal blow behind his back when he least expected it. His son, expecting to inherit his father's kingdom, was soon killed by the outraged townsfolk who viewed Liongo as a leader and champion of the tribes. Hundreds of years after the giant warlord's death his grave was visited by British archaeologist Bishop Steere who wrote:

> The grave, as I saw it in 1912, was a slight elevation in the ground, which might once have been a barrow. It was roughly marked at the

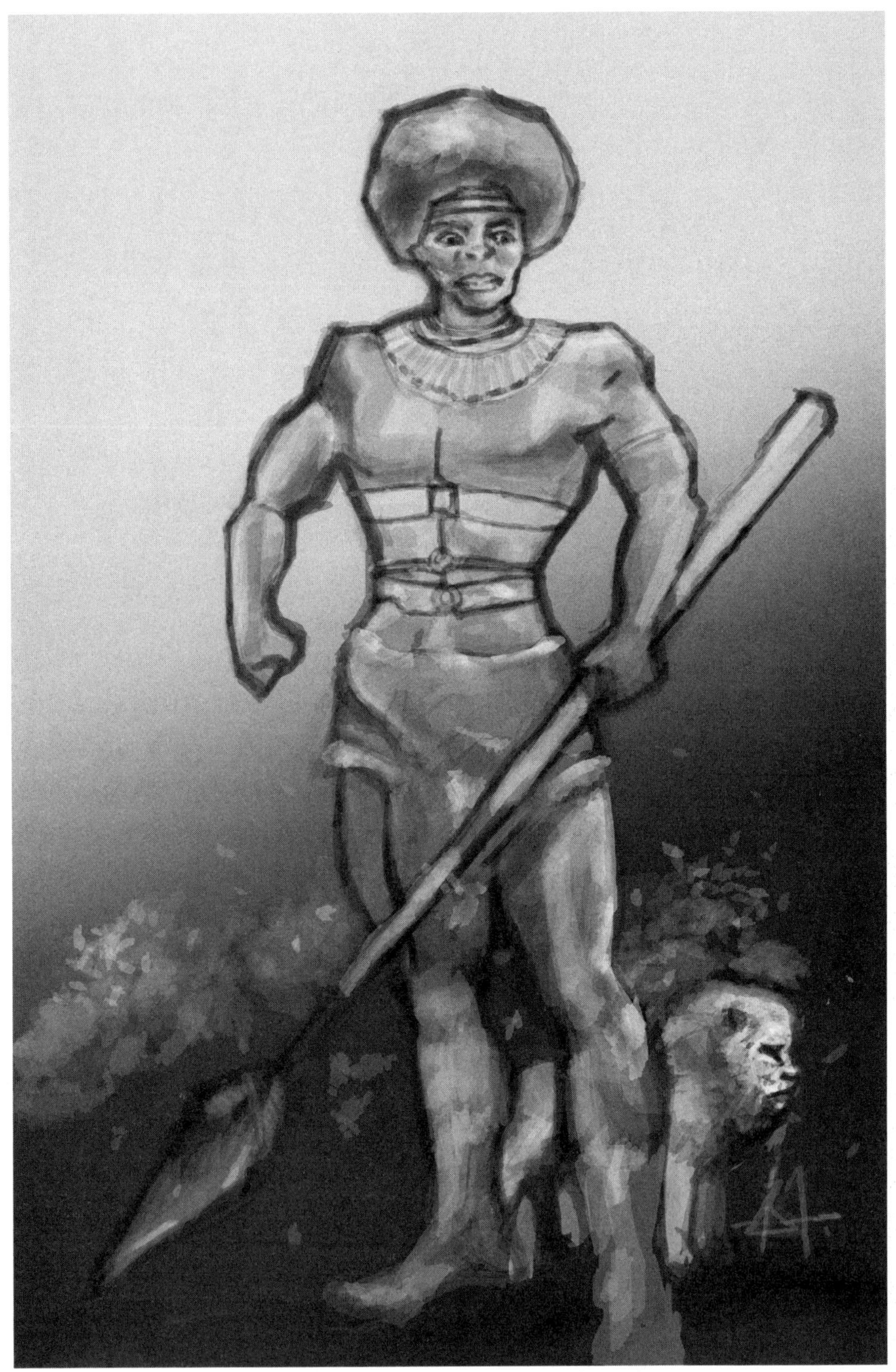

Fig. 8.1. *Liongo*, Bethoven M. Tiano (2016)

> head and foot with rows of white stones, evidently remnants of a complete rectangle. The native overseer in charge of the plantation in which it was situated told me that he and the European superintendent had measured the grave some time before, and found its length from east to west to be "fourteen paces"—some twelve or fourteen yards, suggesting that Liongo might, indeed, have been a giant.[6]

Traces of African giants can also be found in the remote lands of down under where the dark-skinned tribes of the Aborigines speak openly about a mysterious lost race that once inhabited the globe. There has even been some new research suggesting aboriginal Australians and Pacific islanders share a small percentage of genetic material with an unknown ancient hominid. Could these mysterious DNA markings be related to the lost race of giants?

CHAPTER 9

Ancient Giants of Australia, New Zealand, and Pacific Islands

I am convinced of the validity of contradiction. There are many worlds. Each is true, at its time, in its own fashion.

Errol Flynn

MAORI LEGENDS OF NEW ZEALAND

The lands down under hold vast resources of lost, forgotten, and mostly overlooked ancient history. The Aborigine tribes speak of alien visitors, lost cultures, mysterious monsters, and of course ancient giants. In the 1875 edition of the *Timaru Herald,* we can read about some of these ancient New Zealand giants:

> A very large skeleton was found yesterday, about 7 feet below the surface of the sand on the Saltwater Creek spit. Mr. Bullock, the carter, in removing some sand for building purposes, dropped across this relic of a past age and brought the fragments to town. We have had an opportunity of inspecting them, and were struck by their

> symmetry no less than their great size. They appear to have belonged to a man of gigantic statue; but are so far incomplete as to render it difficult to ascertain the dimensions of his frame. The bones are much decayed, a fact which taken in connection with the dryness of the situation where they were found, probably indicates for them a great antiquity.[1]

The skull of this giant was supposedly big enough to hold the skull of a normal human just in its mouth alone. According to local Maori legend these giants were known as the Te Kahui Tipua and had perished in a great flood ages ago. Most of the discovered giant bones were found in New Zealand around the vicinity of the city of Timaru. Numerous reports of these giant skeletons of the Te Kahui Tipua were found up into the twentieth century. However, as in most cases, the bones have all gone missing, and all we are left with are the initial reports of their discovery, like the giant bones found in a cave near Port Waikato, about an hour's boat ride south of Auckland. This story was kept alive by an article in *N.Z. Truth* dated September 29, 1965, with the headline of "Caves Could Reveal Secret of Tall Maoris."[2] This pair of giant Maori skeletons has also mysteriously vanished.

AUSTRALIA'S DREAMTIME GIANTS

According to indigenous Australian beliefs, the giants of the Dreamtime were a race of giant hominids that roamed the Australian continent long before the appearance of the first Aborigines. Australia is also home to twenty-thousand-year-old human footprints, and just recently Cretaceous dinosaur tracks were found on Broome's Cable beach in Western Australia. As for the ancient Australian giants, they are survived by their massive stone tools, giant molars, and the monstrous footprints they left fossilized in the rocks.

In New South Wales, the fossil of an Australian giant was discovered near Bathurst, alongside huge stone tools and hand-axes of tremendous weight and size. The fossicker that discovered the ancient haul believed the bones belonged to somebody that could have been up to twelve feet tall. This discovery reaffirms the Aborigines' belief that a giant race of tool-wielding hominids preceded them on the Australian continent by thousands of years. Rogue Australian archaeologist Rex Gilroy writes about these mysterious Aussie giants in his 1995 book, *Mysterious Australia*.

> I found among other tools a great club weighing 21 lbs. displaying a handle chipped out to form a gripping surface and thumb rest for a mighty hand larger than any living man's. By now I had not the slightest doubt that a race of giant hominids once occupied the Australian continent. Pondering these finds I asked myself if these sites represented three tool-type developmental phases in the history of the race of giant men, or did they represent three distinct races of giants? Over the following months I numbered other sites, and at one of these, site 5, I recovered a huge hand-axe, 25 lbs. in weight, which makes it the heaviest stone artifact yet found at Bathurst. . . . Estimates for the actual size of these men range from 10 to 12 ft. tall and over, weighing anything from 500 to 600 pounds or more. There were, however, even taller giants. From fossiliferous deposits north of bed 3 site 1, I excavated from a depth of 6 ft. below the surface a fossil lower back molar tooth measuring 67 mm. in length by 50 mm. times 42 mm across the crown. From a reconstruction of the probable size of the original jaw from which this molar tooth came we arrive at a complete jaw of approximately 42 cms. in length, 36 cms. wide and with a depth of about 90 cm. The Cranium must therefore have been 60 cm. in length across the dome, by 21 cm. depth. Thus, the complete skull must have been 110cm. depth, about 36 cm. wide and 60 cm. in length. Of course I wish my readers to regard these measurements as nothing more than suppositions. But, if my measurements are approximately correct, the enormous beast to whom this hypothetical skull belongs to would have been at least 25 ft. tall, weighing well over 1,000 lbs![3]

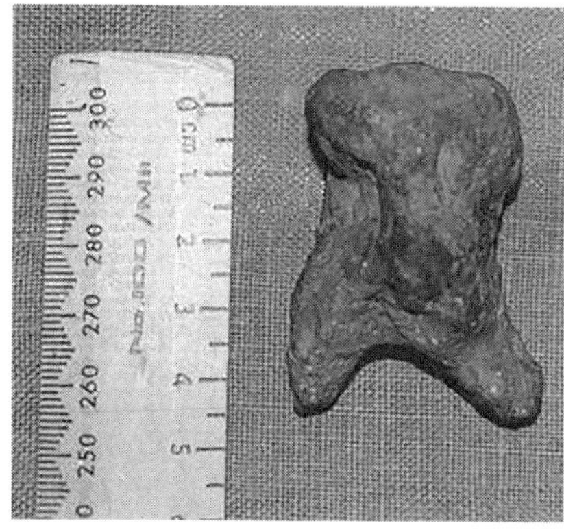

Fig. 9.1. Giant hominid molar (photo by Rex Gilroy, 2012)

French sailors discovered a tribe of "formidable giants" on Shark Bay in Western Australia in 1803. Historian Shino Konishi recounts the French sailors' terrifying encounter with the giants, thanks to the ship's zoologist and chronicler, François Péron, who documented the odd encounter. Konishi writes, "These giants (there were a hundred or more) carried great shields and enormous spears; long, black beards grew down to the middle of their chests; they ran like furies along the beach, brandishing their weapons; they uttered great, long cries and threatened [the] fishermen, who fled precipitately toward the ship." Péron himself recalled that, "the most ancient chronicles that we possess concerning this part of New Holland [or "Australia" as we tend to call it these days] portray it as inhabited by a race of formidable giants."[4]

PACIFIC ISLAND GIANTS

In the winter of 1899 *Austin's Hawaiian Weekly* published a story about giants. This one pertained to an eight-foot-tall-Hawaiian chief, who was interviewed by the daring travel writer Miles Austin.

> The ancient hermit reclined comfortably upon his pile of bones, telling me tales of Hawaiian folklore which, under less distressing circumstances no doubt I should have found instructive, while I crouched upon the rock close to the precipice which formed the

back wall of the hut. At last mine host said it was time we entered the cave. "That rock you are sitting upon stops the entrance." He picked a long stick, evidently for this purpose, and used it as a lever to pry the rock away from the precipitous wall. The rock was so evenly balanced on rolling boulders that it easily swung out into the room, disclosing the entrance to the cave, which was about three feet square. "I hope you have good nerves," said the hermit, as he busied himself preparing a flaming torch made from kukui nut oil. "You will see a great many skeletons, but, of course, being a doctor, human bones cannot have much terror for you." "Yes; I have done a great deal of dissecting in my time," I answered as bravely as I could. We had to crawl in on our hands and knees to enter the cave, but once having entered, we were able to stand erect without difficulty, and in some places the roof was perhaps eight or nine feet high. The faint roar of water could be heard in the deep recesses of the cavern, which, my guide explained, was the underground channel of the spring which caused the little oasis in the rocky desert. On either side of the cave, laid out on ledges or benches hewed out of the solid rock, were hundreds of skeletons that looked ghastly in the feeble light of the torch. The floor of the cave was strewn with loose bones, and it was impossible to avoid making football of the skulls as we walked along. Mine host chattered pleasantly, even cheerfully as we went, called this or that giant chief's skeleton by name, relating anecdotes of his life and deeds of valor. It was doubtless very interesting and instructive, but I must confess that I felt very uncomfortable. . . . We had proceeded perhaps fifty yards or more, when my ancient guide stopped and turned around so as to face me. Reaching to the ledge on the left, he selected the shin-bone of one of the largest skeletons in the cave. "What a giant this fellow must have been," he said. "Surely not less than eight feet tall."[5]

The Solomon Islands, an island archipelago near Papa New Guinea in the South Pacific, also has an interesting history of giants, with aston-

Fig. 9.2. *Japanese Soldiers Encounter a Solomon Island Giant,* Brian Snoddy (2016)

ishing tales both ancient and modern. According to local reports, and the research of writers like Marius Boirayon and Jonathan Gray, it's said that giants still live inside the vast cave systems running underneath the rain forest mountain ranges of Guadalcanal. Could these accounts of modern giants be true?

Ezekiel Alebua, the former prime minister and previous premier of Guadalcanal recounted how when he was a child his father took him to a cave in east Guadalcanal to see the burial remains of a giant skeleton that was at least fifteen feet in length. Author of *Dead Men's Secrets* Jonathan Gray writes:

> To the local population on Guadalcanal, giants are common knowledge. Interaction with giants has been frequent through their history. The giant's territory is a 1,000-square-kilometre area of mountains covered in tropical jungle west of Mount Popomanaseu. Local tribes, not only in Guadalcanal, but in most parts of the Solomon Islands have recorded a tumultuous historical relationship with the giants. The area is rich in memories of such encounters. Giants allegedly still survive on Santa Isabel Island. Although they are fewer in number than on Guadalcanal, there are two areas where they live. Any local person is able to steer you in the right direction.

> Another of the Solomon Islands is Choiseul. The island of Choiseul is not small. Some 300 kilometres long by 80 kilometres wide, with numerous villages. But there is one large area of its interior where no village exists. And apparently with good reason . . . living giants. In the Kwara'ee region, north of there, is a large burial place scattered with giant skeletons. They lie all over the ground. In a nearby village stands a hut, one of whose main support poles is a human femur bone nearly 8 feet long![6]

The mountain ranges of Guadalcanal have been attracting prospectors since the 1970s when gold was first discovered there. By the late '90s the Ross Mining Company had a monopoly over the local gold-digging business and were in the process of bulldozing an area in northern Guadalcanal when one of their huge bulldozers broke down. Leaving the ten-ton blade behind, the workers hauled the bulldozer back to the workshop and promptly called it a night. The next morning, when bulldozer and crew returned to the site, they were astonished to find that the ten-ton blade had vanished! Everyone on the team was in disbelief. How could such a heavy object vanish without a trace? A search party for the blade was soon organized, and after about twenty minutes one of the workers discovered a trail of giant human footprints leading up to a small hill with a cave entrance opening. The footprints ended near the base of a cave, and the mammoth blade was discovered discarded about a hundred feet away.

These were the same living giants that former Guadalcanal premier and finance minister Victor Ngele encountered during a scouting expedition on Gold Ridge. Due to bad weather and a slippery road, their Toyota Hilux 4WD truck bogged down off the road in the mud. With their vehicle unmovable, Ngele and his companions made the trek back to the nearest village for help. When they returned they were surprised to find their Toyota back on the road, but even more shocked to see two giant fifteen-feet-tall men standing on each end of the muddied truck. In fear, everyone scrambled away from the Toyota, with the giants dashing into the forest and Ngele and his crew returning the way they came. About a half hour later, after summoning the courage to return to the site, Ngele examined the giant footprints and determined that the two giants had picked up the truck and placed it safely back on the road.

Any giant-seeking adventurer might want to book a trip to the Solomon Islands in the near future and do some firsthand investigating into the fascinating possibility that some members of that lost race of giants are still alive. For even more adventures into the mysterious, you can take a day's flight over the endless blue Pacific until landing on Easter Island, home of those enigmatic giant stone head statues known as the Maoi. Some of these massive megalithic statues have recently been shown to have bodies as well. The archaeologists from UCLA who discovered them were blown away by the long Maoi bodies resting under ten feet of Easter Island dirt. The bodies even showed strange undeciphered petroglyphs and intricately carved symbols. Could these towering Maoi statues have been built by the ancient giants of Easter Island?

Fig. 9.3. Megalithic stone masonry at Ahu Vinapu, Easter Island (photo by Signalhead, 2009)

Fig. 9.4. Close-up of mortarless masonry at Ahu Vinapu, Easter Island (photo by Koppas, 2009)

Fig. 9.5. Megalithic ruins of Easter Island (photo by Valeria 04, 2009)

According to explorer Carl Friedrich Behrens, a member of the Dutch expedition led by Jacob Roggeveen to Easter Island in 1722, when they approached the island they were greeted by giant natives more than twelve feet high! Behrens gives a firsthand report of this encounter, saying, "With truth, I might say that these savages are all of more than gigantic size. The men are tall and broad in proportion, averaging

12 feet in height. Surprising as it may appear, the tallest men on board of our ship could pass between the legs of these children of Goliath without bending the head."[7] This account plus the colossal stone statues add weight to the presence of giants on Easter Island. There is also a massive megalithic stone wall with masonry so fine that it reminds one of the megalithic structures in Peru and Egypt. Usually when there are tales of ancient giants in a certain area you can also find prehistoric megalithic stoneworks within the vicinity of the legends.

As for their counterparts in Australia, it seems that those giants have since all but vanished. And the lands of down under remain more notable for their extreme remoteness, Crocodile Dundee, boxing kangaroos, shark attacks, and the miles of endless beaches that surfers dream upon.

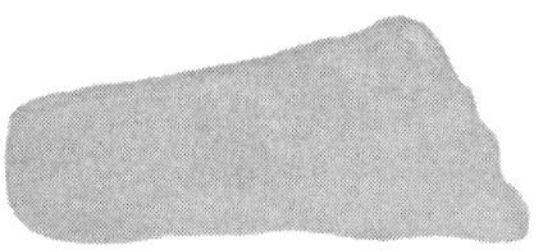

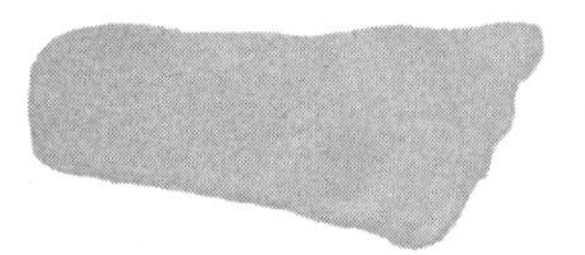

CHAPTER 10

Ancient Giants of East Asia

What you seek is seeking you.

Rumi

CHINA'S CORRIDOR OF GIANTS

Three undeniable facts about Chinese civilization are: its secluded culture, its enormous landmass, and its vast number of people. The three have a profound effect on the collective knowledge referred to as Chinese history. China is a closed society. A sign of their internal caste system was "The Forbidden City" (now tourist city)—the imperial palace of the Ming and Qing Dynasties circa 1420, where only royalty and their guests were allowed, much like today's Buckingham Palace. Hence, the name "Forbidden" given to this vast housing complex built to accommodate emperors and their extended families. Interaction, even within a defined area, was determined by status and wealth. Limited exchange within groups, limited information, and only a small number of the population held the most power. Under communist rule today, China remains no different than it was back then, a closed and strict society.

In ancient times China's view of the world was from this isolationist perspective, which held that the Chinese empire was the center of global civilization and the emperor the leader of the civilized world, while all others were considered lesser vassals or barbarian invaders. But during the reign of Emperor Wu of Han (r. 141–87 BCE) China began to establish relations among other Asian territories through the envoy Xhang Qian. Qian was given a mission to seek an alliance with the Yuezhi people, an ancient Indo-European tribe of Central Asia, against the Xiongnu, a coalition of nomadic people that included the Huns, and who populated the eastern Asian steppe from the third century BCE to the first century CE. While on the diplomatic mission, Qian was taken prisoner by Huns upon reaching the Hexi Corridor (or Gansu Corridor), an ancient and historical area that extended from northwest central Asia toward the southeast. He was held for ten years before he was able to escape across the Gobi Desert and the Pamirs and arrive at his destination, where the alliance was refused on the grounds it was useless. The distance was too great to be effective.

On the long return home Qian was again captured by Huns and again detained, this time for a year. Through his imprisonment Qian was exposed to the geography and the culture of nearby tribes. He made a second, more extended journey to the western regions and sent further envoys to Daway, Hotan, Da Yuezhi, Anxi (now Iran), Juandu (India), and other countries. While the goal of the original mission of alliance didn't materialize, Zhang Qian created a network of interconnection with peoples of distant lands that further developed the Hexi Corridor, which eventually became the northern part of the Silk Road. It is in this corridor that the ancient myths and legends of giants and dragons, dinosaurs, and prehistoric bones are to be found.

This distant society of enormous size, separated from the Westernized world geographically and through several languages, has passed down its ancient folklore and myths where truthful historical and cultural information can be found. Among several creation myths it's interesting that the legend of Pangu[1] is familiar to all Chinese people. In this Chinese creation myth, a giant is the source and protagonist. It

Fig. 10.1. *Pangu* (1897)

is an ancient tale. For need of a firm date, historians have credited its origin to author Zu Zheng of the third century CE because he was the first to write it down. The myth, similar to the Bible story of creation, begins with nothing, void, amid which Pangu is born out of a big black egg. He is said to have slept for eighteen thousand years, during which the ying and yang were formed. When he awoke he held the two apart. As he did so he became bigger, stretching the distance between heaven and earth by ten feet per day as he grew. After another eighteen thousand years Pangu died and his body became different parts of the universe, his eyes became the sun and moon, his corpse created Earth, and the parasites that infected his body became humans. It's ironic that human behavior on its living host planet is of a parasitic nature.[1]

In Asian scriptures, legends, and myths, there is plenty of material that gives clues to an era of fifteen-foot-tall giants that once walked those lands. One of the earliest accounts to reach the West came about during the Jesuit missions of the fifteenth century. Needless to say, these missions met with resistance and failure since the Jesuits sought to indoctrinate China in the same way they had colonized and dominated other lands. Size was not an issue for the Jesuits. They'd already encountered huge lands and managed to infiltrate their culture and twist the customs to suit Catholicism just the same. However, the Chinese were different. They were more civilized than Europe. Melchior Nunnez Barreto was one of these Jesuits. He traveled extensively into the Canton Province of China in 1555 and lived among the Chinese. It wasn't until he was in India that he wrote letters that specifically described the guardians of the gate of Peking as giants. Historically, Chinese emperors at times had giants who served in their personal guard or as archers. Other missionaries such as George Hakeman reported the same thing, and Samuel Purchas in 1625 described seeing a Chinese warrior giant.[2] To this day, people from that area are taller than most average humans; take for instance Chang Woo Gow, a giant man who was over eight feet tall and who became famous for traveling to England and visiting the royal family in 1860 (see fig. 10.2).

Fig. 10.2. Chang the Chinese giant
(*Harpers Weekly*, 1865)

One of the most fascinating discoveries made early last century was that of a giant mummy enclosed in a large, square coffin that was exhibited at the Aisho exposition in Japan in 1915.[3] The mummy was obtained by a Japanese explorer while visiting a Buddhist temple in the province of Kiangsi, and it's believed to be that of a famous monk who lived in China at the beginning of the Christian era. The mummy is eight feet high, and while this may not sound like much, it was an odd enough size that was impressive for an exhibition.

Today anthropologists have proved that giants really did exist in remote Chinese history. The remains uncovered in areas of southern China and Java give evidence of men whose average height was more than eleven feet tall. In 2003 archaeologist Liao Zhaoyu discovered "long, boat-shaped wooden coffins" in the Xinjiang Uygur province of southern China. Liao was the director of the institute of the Culture of the Western Region at Tarim University in Alar. After the discovery he spoke excitedly with the state news reporter because he believed he had found the remains of the giants talked about in Chinese legends. He called the tomb "Kungang," which is the ancient name of Alar, and the locals named the sand dunes "The Valley of the Giants." Liao described to the reporter:

> [T]he skeleton of the tallest mummy discovered so far is about 2.3 meters, (2.3 m = 7ft $6\frac{35}{64}$ in) and the coffin is about 2.8 meters long (2.8 m = 9ft $2\frac{15}{64}$ in), but medical experts say the man may have been even taller when he was alive: up to 3 inches (7ft $9\frac{35}{64}$ in). In addition to features similar to those of ancient Europeans, such as blond hair and high cheekbones, many of the mummies or skeletons have large frames, more than 2 meters tall.[4]

Granted, these mummies aren't the fifteen-feet-tall guards talked about by the early missionaries, but the Kungang mummies are an indication of people with clearly unusually high stature for the average person of that era. These giants also had golden-colored hair, an unusual trait for the Chinese.

The region is so ancient that even dinosaurs once roamed the Mongolian desert! On September 30, 2016, Professor Shinobu Ishigaki of Okayama University of Science discovered in the Gobi Desert one of the biggest dinosaur footprints that has ever been unearthed.[5] The dinosaur footprint was found in a geologic layer formed between seventy to ninety million years ago, according to researchers. While this is a dinosaur and not a giant, it is an example of how today, perhaps thanks to technology, there is an ongoing cooperation among cultures in order to bring these and other forthcoming fascinating revelations to light.

GIANT TRACES IN MALAYSIA AND THE PHILIPPINES

In Batu, Maung, in the state of Penang, Malaysia, there is a Chinese temple named Sam Poh Footprint Temple.[6] The local Chinese fishermen here pay respects to the temple every day before going to sea. The temple was built in 1993, but what's intriguing about it is that there's a footprint mark stamped on solid rock that is more than one hundred years old. The size of the footprint is thirty-three inches, and the local people believe the footprint belongs to Sang Gedembai, a giant said to have been strong and feared by the locals. According to one version, a villager who was chopping wood caused a piece to fly into the giant's eye. The giant ran away terrified, leaving footprints that are still visible today. They call the footprint "Tapak Gedembai" and say this is one of four footprints left by Sang Gedembai. The others are in Pulau island, Aman island, and Bayan Lepans; all are relatively close to the temple in Batu, Maung.

The tribal people of the hinterlands of the Philippines, Agusan, Bohol, and Bukidnon have found ancient skulls with only one eyeball socket, similar to the cyclops, the one-eyed giants popular in Greek mythology. The skulls were found in limestone caves in Mount Palaupau in Bohol, in Sumilao, Bukidnon, and in parts of Agusan. News of the discovery of these giant skulls prompted the National Museum to launch an excavation in Bohol and they also found one such cyclops skull. Archaeologist Rey Santiago, acknowledging the overall age of the bones, said, "Intensive study on the skull showed it belonged to an ancient settler." However, Santiago said his theory of the one-eye socket was that it could have been caused by a limestone chemical reaction, creating a new eyeball socket: "Human bones and limestone have similar (composition)."[7] The question with this theory is, why is the eye socket part of the skeleton, and specifically why near the eyes? Why not the cranium?

Not surprisingly, even after the scientific explanation by the archaeologists of the National Museum, the locals continue to maintain that in ancient times there were two races of giants. One was the Kapre, who were thought to be evil, and the other the one-eyed giants who were considered heroes. Ancient folklore claims giants once lived in the plains of Central and Northern Mindanao, and according to a popular legend in Bukidnon, Agyo was one of those giants. The legend talks about Agyo fighting against the Spanish conquistadors. The tribe worships the figure of Agyo and say they are keeping the bones in a sacred cave.

JAPAN'S GIANT ARTIFACTS

The longest ancient Japanese sword ever unearthed has been rescued from a sixth-century underground tomb on Japan's southernmost island of Kyushu in the Miyazaki Prefecture.[8] The sword in its remaining state is approximately 142 centimeters, but according to researchers, once it is fully restored its estimated length would reach well over 150 centimeters [five feet] long. It matches other Japanese giant artifacts, which used to be displayed at the Tokyo National Museum before being buried deep somewhere in the museum's basement.

Artist and Japanese historian Brian Snoddy writes about these giant artifacts after seeing them for the first time in 2002:

> Although I had visited before, I was now shocked at what I saw, and was dumbfounded that I had not noticed these things before. I saw several objects that were so large in proportion to Japanese people at that time, they can only be described as "giant artifacts." The first objects to receive my attention were some spear points. They were included in a display of 12 objects altogether. Four of the objects were KA blades. A KA is a type of pole axe, where

> the spear-like blade was attached to the side of a shaft, and used in a chopping and hooking fashion. There were 2 spear points so large that it made me do a double take. They were both double the size of the next largest object in the display, and measured about 3 feet in length. . . . All of these objects are about 3 times the size of regular sword fittings. Most swords of this time were single-edged, straight swords that carried a cutting-blade length of 2 to 3 feet. However these "giant" sword parts could have easily supported a cutting blade length of 6 to 8 feet. Figure number 5 of the illustration, in my opinion, shows one of the most impressive pieces of the "giant artifacts" in the museum. It is an iron shield about 5 feet tall. Made of several riveted iron plates, it is a magnificent piece of craftsmanship. In the display, this shield is seated between 2 suits of armor. The armors are so small in comparison, the shield looks like a large door. The weight would be anyone's guess, but I suspect at least 30 pounds. How a 5 foot person could carry this thing around during hand-to-hand combat is beyond me . . . I also could not imagine anyone under 8 feet high wearing these things either. As of 2009, my last visit to Japan, all the remaining objects were still there. However, I have not heard nor read anything from any museum worker or any Japanese historian who can or has explained the giant nature of these artifacts. They are simply ignored.[9]

On a misty fall morning in the Chinese village of Pingyan, a group of travelers came across a giant footprint measuring 57 centimeters [almost two feet] long, 20 centimeters wide, and 3 centimeters deep.[10] More of these giant footprints can be found thousands of miles away in the ancient lands of mystical India, a country with an astonishing history and fabulous tales of ancient giants.

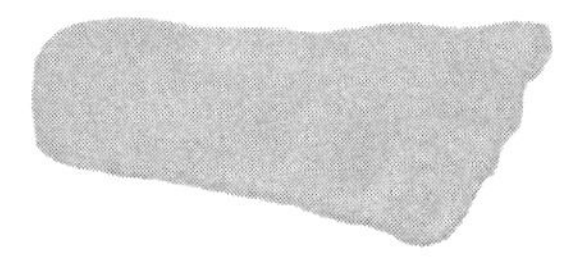

CHAPTER 11

Ancient Giants of India

As the heat of a fire reduces wood to ashes, the fire of knowledge burns to ashes all karma.

Lord Krishna

In 2015 archaeologists in India discovered a group of skeletons from one of the world's most ancient empires, findings that provide clues about the first human settlements of the Indus Valley Civilization, which appeared around five thousand years ago.[1] This was a civilization that extended across India, modern-day Pakistan, and the northeast of Afghanistan. The skeletons were found in a graveyard at Rakhigarhi village in Hisar, a site near the 1934 discovery of a massive ancient giant skeleton as reported in the August 10, 1934, edition of *The Argus:*

Giant Prehistoric Ape—Skeleton
31½ ft. long found

> The sensational discovery of a skeleton believed to be a prehistoric giant ape, measuring 31 feet 6 inches in length, is reported from Jubbulpore. The discovery was made by a farmer who noticed a bone protruding from the sand on the river bank near the village

> of Jaintiha. Attempts to dislodge the skeleton with the aid of other villagers failed, whereupon the chief of the State had the skeleton dug out. Three men were required to lift it, the legs alone measuring 10 feet. The skeleton has been placed in the palace of the chief pending examination by geologists, among whom the discovery has created enormous interest. The Jubbulpore district is renowned for its wealth of fossilized relics of an earlier age, the last important discovery three years ago being the remains of a giant prehistoric mammal reputed to be centuries old.[2]

Some believed these bones to be those of Hanuman, the giant monkey god of Hindu legend. He also left his footprints throughout India, or at least some sort of giant humanoid being did. One of these four-foot-long footprints, which would also make the giant over thirty feet tall, can be seen at a temple in Lepakshi, a small village in Andhra Pradesh.[3] Some Hindu and Jain sects believe that Hanuman was not a real ape but a humanlike giant with slight physical variations. Sacred texts from many ancient civilizations describe these giants as hybrids between gods and humans. As we have seen, in the Bible they are called Nephilim. Hanuman can also be classified as a Nephilim because his father was a god and his mother was human.

According to Hindu scriptures, Hanuman was not the only giant that looked like an ape; a whole race of giant apes called the Vanara was documented. Is it possible that this huge skeleton is one of these apelike gods? What happened to Hanuman's skeleton? Today, we are not able to trace the whereabouts of the thirty-two-foot Rakhigarhi skeleton anywhere. Since India was under British control at that time, this priceless evidence was possibly taken to England, along with many other rare artifacts, and lost down the memory hole like most of the other bones we've discussed so far.

There are repeated mentions of these giants in the Hindu holy texts called the Puranas. According to Indian mythology, Brahma created people of such incredible size that large trees were easily uprooted by

Fig. 11.1. Hanuman the monkey god
(image by Kru Tony Moore, 2013)

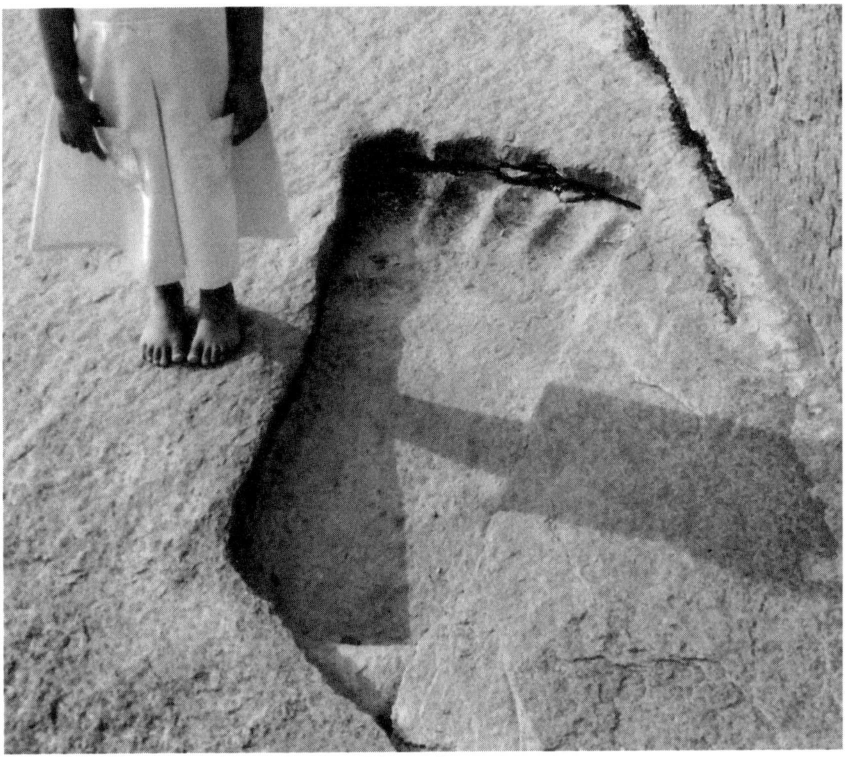

Fig. 11.2. Giant footprint at Lepakshi Temple
(photo by Vu2sga, 2012)

Fig. 11.3. Giant footprint at Lepakshi Temple 2
(photo by Pponnada, 2009)

them once they put their hands around the trunk. The purpose of creating them was to bring order to the world and to also stop the fighting and wicked practices among men. Bhima, mentioned in the Indian epic *Mahabharata,* happened to be one of the god-sons of Brahma and he also had similar powers and a giant frame. One of the sons of Bhima, Ghatotkacha, was a giant.

In the Indian epic *Ramayana,* the chief of the three supreme Hindu gods, Vishnu, was incarnated in a noble family. He fought and defeated the giant Kumbhakarna, the brother of Ravana and Ravana himself, king of the giant rakshasas (demons), whose kingdom was in Sri Lanka.

Sri Lanka, already a mysterious and ancient country, is an island off the coast of southern India, rich with tales of ancient giants. Ten of them once served in the council of the Dutugemunu the Great.[4] The giant warrior Nandimitra was considered the strongest Sri Lankan in history and was sent to fight for the Sri Lankan king at the battle of Kahagalagama to secure independence. History records that only two of the original ten giants survived this battle. Possible footprints of these giants can be seen at Adams Peak in central Sri Lanka.

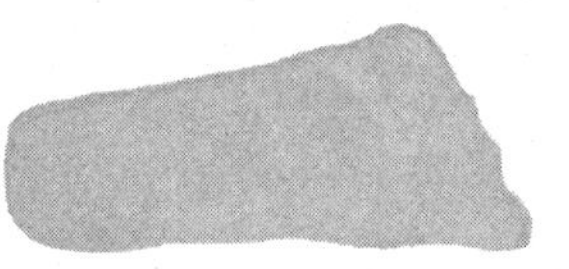

CONCLUSION

There *Were* Giants on the Earth!

The monumental stoneworks of the ancient world bear mute witness to the giants who quarried, transported, and placed the megaliths to construct awe-inspiring temples, fortresses, astronomical sites, sculptures, graves, and monuments to the dead.

But all the evidence of the giants is not mute. From the Bible's specific listing of thirty-six tribes and twenty-two individual giants in the ancient Holy Land, to dramatic Greek legends, to the folklore of the Solomon Islands, the stories told by peoples around the globe attest to the presence of giants living, building, fighting, and ruling throughout the ancient world. Despite the vast differences in cultures in places as disparate as Russia and Africa, the British Isles and the Hawaiian Islands, Spain and New Zealand, France and India, and beyond, they have all preserved memories of ancient giants.

In addition, around the world, the impressive remains of giants have been found preserved under stone and earth, sometimes accompanied by giant-sized weapons. Despite the all-too-common "habit" of academia to "lose" or rebury those remains in museum catacombs, the documentation of their discoveries in the popular press is widespread. One wonders at the academic resistance to acknowledging the existence of our larger forebears: Is it because modern egos recoil from the idea that anything bigger or better could have come before? Is this a form of species arrogance: not allowing any disturbance to the story line that current humans are the victorious culmination of "survival of the fittest"? Or is it due to a fundamental dis-ease with visions of humanity too unlike what we know?

Whatever the reason, for all the traces of ancient giants preserved in the human psyche and in the earth, there are almost as many instances of cover-ups and dismissals. But, as you have seen, when the records that have not been erased are gathered together, as they are here, they constitute evidence that is not easily dismissed, especially when they are paired with the abundant and pervasive oral history of giants and their still visible monumental creations.

If you haven't already, I encourage you to use this book to guide your explorations of the rich treasure trove of legends and folklore of giants from around the world, further research the remains of giants, or visit the inspiring and wonder-inducing megalithic sites. It is sure to be a gigantic adventure!

Fig. A.1. *The Book of Giants*, Bethoven M. Tiano (2016)

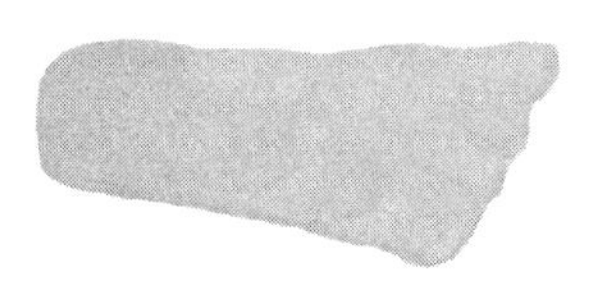

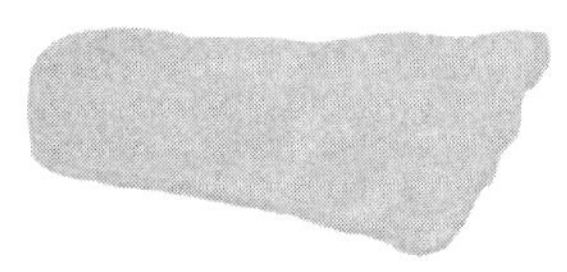

APPENDIX

Finding the *Book of Giants*

The *Book of Giants* is an antediluvian narrative that tells of the background and fate of the Nephilim in the flood. It has long been known as a work that circulated among the Manicheans as a composition attributed to their founding prophet, Mani (ca. 216–276 CE). However, the earliest known traditions for the book originate in Aramaic copies of a *Book of Giants* in the Dead Sea Scrolls.

During the twentieth century a number of finds have shed considerable light on the literary evidence for the *Book of Giants*. The discoveries and publications of Manichaen fragments from the *Book of Giants* discovered at Turfan have substantiated the many references to its circulation among, and use by, the Manicheans. Further identification of the Manichean *Book of Giants* was revealed in 1971 when J. T. Milik discovered several Aramaic fragments of Enochic works among the Dead Sea Scrolls. The three Books of Enoch are ancient Jewish religious texts, not part of the biblical canon, attributed to Noah's great grandfather, Enoch. The fragmentary scrolls discovered by Milik were clearly the primary source utilized by Mani in the compilation of his book and confirmed the *Book of Giants* as an independent composition from the second temple period.

The *Book of Giants* expands the narrative of the birth of the giants in Genesis 6.1–4. In this story, the giants came into being when the sons of God had sexual intercourse with mortal women who birthed a hybrid race of giants. These giants partook in destructive and immoral actions, which devastated humanity. When Enoch heard of this, he was distressed and asked God to bring judgment to the giants. In his mercy, God chose to give the giants a chance to repent by transmitting dreams to two giants named Ohyah and Hahyah, who relayed the dreams to an assembly of giants. The giants were perplexed with the dreams, so they sent a giant named Mahaway to Enoch's abode. Enoch interceded on their behalf and gave tablets to the giants with the meaning of the dreams and God's future judgment. When the giants heard this, many chose to act in defiance to God.

While the Qumran fragments were incomplete at this point, the Manichean fragments tell of the hosts of God subduing the race of giants through battle. What follows is an article written by W. B. Henning about the *Book of Giants,* originally published in the *Bulletin of the School of Oriental and African Studies*, University of London, Vol. XI, Part 1, 1943, 52–74, and available online at http://www.sacred-texts.com/chr/giants/giants.htm#.

The article concludes with translations of the found fragments, but the transcriptions of the original texts have been omitted in the version reproduced here.

The Book of the Giants

W. B. Henning

ISAAC DE BEAUSOBRE, the Huguenot author of one of the best books ever written on Manichæism (*Histoire critique de Manichée et du Manicheïsme*, Amsterdam, 1734, 1739), was the one to make the only sound suggestions on the sources used by Mani for the compilation of his *Book of the Giants,* the Book of Enoch, and the *Γραφὴ τῶν Γιγάντων,* which Kenan, a great-grandson of Noah, discovered lying in a field (vol. i, 429, n. 6). The latter work has been identified by Alfaric (*Les Écritures Manichéennes*, ii, 32) with a book whose contents are briefly indicated in the *Decretum Gelasianum,* p. 54, ll. 298–9 (ed. Dobschütz): *Liber de Ogia*[1] *nomine gigante qui post diluvium cum dracone ab hereticis pugnasse perhibetur apocryphus.* Of the Book of Enoch, which was composed in the Hebrew language in the second century BCE, only an Ethiopic version, a few Greek fragments, and some excerpts made by the Byzantine chronographer Georgius Syncellus survive.[2] Mani, who could hardly read the Hebrew, must have used an Aramaic edition based directly on the Hebrew text (see below, *Šhmyz'd*). He quotes mainly from the first part, which Georgius S. (p. 45, Fl.-R.) calls "the first book of Enoch on the Egrēgoroi," but shows himself acquainted also with the subsequent chapters.[3]

It is noteworthy that Mani, who was brought up and spent most of his life in a province of the Persian empire, and whose mother[4]

1. Numerous variants (p. 126, Dobschütz), e.g. *de ogiae, de oggie, diogiae, diogine, diogenes, de ozia, de ugia, de ugica, de ogiga, de eugia, de uegia, de eugenia,* and so forth. In Migne's *Patrologia Latina* the text is in vol. 59, 162–63.

2. See Charles, *The Book of Enoch,* 2nd ed., 1912. For the Greek fragments (and Georgius S.) the edition by Flemming and Radermacher (= *Fl.-R.*) is quoted here. For Mani's use of the Enoch literature see my papers in *Sb.P.A.W.*, 1934, 27–32, and in *ZDMG.*, 90, 2–4.

3. See below A 86–94, and compare G 19–21 with Enoch 67, 4, and G 38 with Enoch 17, 1; 21, 7; 54, 6; 67, 4–13. On chaps. 72 sqq. see *Sb.P.A.W.*, 1934, 32.

4. Namely the Kamsarakan-k' (mentioned often in the Armenian history of the fourth century) who claimed descent from the royal house of the Arsacids. This is clear from the Chinese-Manichæan text that preceded the *Fragment Pelliot,* now printed in the Taishô Tripiṭaka but hitherto untranslated: "He was born in the country of Sulin (= Babylonia), in the royal abode of B'uât-tiei (= Patī-g), by his wife Muân-i̯äm (= Maryam) of the family of Ki̯əm-sât-g'i̯ɒn (= Kamsar(a)gān)." The name Κάρασσα in the Byzantine formula of abjuration (Migne, *Patr. Gr.*, i, 1468) may be corrupted from Kamsar-. Thus there is a grain of truth in the assertion in the *K. al-Fihrist,* 327, 31, that Mani's mother had belonged to the Arsacid house: Maryam (ed, Marmaryam) is given as one of her names.—It is not proposed to discuss the origin of Mani's father here.

belonged to a famous Parthian family,[5] did not make any use of the Iranian mythological tradition. There can no longer be any doubt that the Iranian names of *Sām, Narīmān,* and so forth, which appear in the Persian and Sogdian versions of the *Book of the Giants,* did not figure in the original edition, written by Mani in the Syriac language.[6] His disciples, who, it is well known, were in the habit of translating every word of a text (including the names of months, deities, etc.), seen fit also to "translate" the names of the giants. Thus *Sām* is merely the translation of *Ohya*. However, they kept some of the original names (e.g. *Šhmyz'd*), and adapted some others (e.g. *Wrwgd'd*).[7]

The story of the fallen angels and their giant sons needed little adaptation to be fitted into Mani's system. Of course, the heavenly origin of the *B'nē-hā-Elōhīm*[8] of Genesis vi, 2, 4, the *'Εγρήγοροι*, of the Book of Enoch, did not square with Mani's conviction that no evil could come from good. Therefore he transformed them into "demons," namely those demons that when the world was being constructed had been imprisoned in the skies under the supervision of the *Rex Honoris.* They rebelled and were recaptured, but two hundred of them escaped to the earth. Mani also used the term *'Εγρήγοροι* (preserved in Coptic, see texts L, M, P, S), or rather *'yr* in Aramaic (once in a Middle Persian fragment, text D), but in Eastern sources they are mostly referred to as "demons" (Pers. *dyw'n*, Parth. *dyw'n* in T 6, Sogd. *δywt* in G, H 17, K 7, *cytyt* in E, *δywt ZY ykšyšt* in H. 16).

5. The *Fragment Pelliot,* now printed in the Taishô Tripiṭaka as No. 2141a, vol. 54, p. 1280A.

6. I have abandoned my earlier opinion on this point (*ZDMG.,* 90, 4) which was based on insufficient material. The important Sogdian fragment, text H, was not then known to me.

7. See *BSOS.*, viii, 583; *ZDMG.*, 90, 4. See also Bal. *girōk,* Geiger, No.107.

8. Cf. also Parthian *bgpwhr'n,* Sogd. *βγpšyt,* lit. "sons of God" = angels (also fem. Sogd. *βγpwryšt*). Thus *bgpwhr* has a double meaning in Parthian, it being (Sogd. *βγpwr*) also the translation of Chin. *T'ien-tzŭ,* or rather of Skt. *devaputra.*

The puzzling clause of Genesis 6:4: "The Nephilim were on the earth those days," was interpreted by Mani in this fashion: "when the Egrēgoroi descended, the animals, or proto-animals, were already in existence." Mani confused *nəfīlīm* with *nefäl* (*näfäl*) = *ἔκτρωμα:* see Nöldeke, *ZDMG.*, 43 (1889), 536, who rightly referred to the formula of abjuration (*P.Gr.,* i, 1461) where the giants and the "abortions" are mentioned in one breath. In Manichæan parlance, "abortion" (cf. also MPers. *'bg'ng*, Sogd. *pš'q*) is synonymous with "animal."

We are therefore left with the *Gibbōrīm,* understood by Mani as "giants."[9] He probably used the equivalent Syriac word, *gabbārē* (*gnbr'*), which his disciples translated as *γίγαντες, al-jabābirah* in Arabic, MPers. and Parthian *k'w'n*, Sogd. *kwyšt* = *kawišt* (Sing. *qwy, kw'y* = *kawi*); cf. *Sb.P.A.W.*, 1934, 30. In Sasanian times the words derived from the Avestan *Kavi* were generally understood as "giant"; see Benveniste, *MO.*, xxvi, 214, and Polotsky in *Mir.Man.,* iii, 901. Thus MPers. Parth. *k'w* is freely used in Manichæan texts, e.g. of the Father of Light (M 40), of solar deities, of leading Manichæans (both in *Mir.Man.,* iii), also of the First Man and Ahriman[10] with reference to the First Battle (which therefore could have been described as a *γιγαντομαχία*).[11] However, the

9. Herein he differed from the common interpretation of the passage (Nephilim = giants), shared also by the authors of the Book of Enoch.

10. M 41: *'br q'rc'r 'wṯ zmbg 'stft cy 'whrmyzdbg qyrd 'd dyw'n: dw q'w'n 'wṯ dw nyw'n.*

11. This word, in the anti-Manichæan book by Alexander Lycopolitanus, p. 8, 10, ed. Brinkmann, refers neither to the Manich. "First Battle", nor to Mani's *Book of the Giants,* as Cumont, *Rech.*, i, 3; ii, 160 sq., erroneously states. Cumont goes so far as to say that in the quoted passage Alexander had given a summary of Mani's work, and Benveniste, *MO.*, xxvi, 213, has repeated this statement. In fact, Alexander says that experts in Greek mythology might quote, from the Greek poets, the *Greek γιγαντομαχία*, as a *parallel* to the Manich. doctrine of the rising by the Hyle against God. In ch. 25 (p. 37, 13 sqq.) Alexander explains that such poetical fables about giants could not be regarded as a satisfactory parallel, because they were myths and meant to be understood as allegories. He then (37, 17) quotes the story of Genesis 6:2–4, which he provides with an allegorical explanation. But he ascribes it to the *History of the Jews* without even mentioning the *Book of the Giants.* This shows conclusively that he had no knowledge of Mani's book.

word *k'w* is applied only to men and such beings as are imagined anthropomorphous. Where one would translate *γίγας* as *monster,* the Iranian equivalent is *mzn, Mazan.* Thus the *γίγας τῆς θαλάσσης* (*Kephalaia,* 113 and notes), whose breathing operations are responsible for ebb and flow (cf. also Beruni, *India,* 203, 10–11), is called *Mzn 'y (z)rhyg*[12] in Middle Persian (M 99, V 22–3). Accordingly, MPers. *mzn* (adj.[13] and noun) and the related words, Pahl. *mǎzan, māzanīg,* Sogd. *mzny'n δyw,* Av. *māzainya-,*[14] should be rendered as "monster", or "gigantic, monstrous."

The Egrēgoroi and their giant progeny are fought and vanquished by four archangels: Raphael, Michael, Gabriel, and Istrael (Enoch, 10, 1; or: Uriel, or: Fanuel). In the *Book of the Giants* they are called "the four angels." They are frequently invoked by name in Manichæan prayers (e.g. M 4 d 19, f 6; M 20), as *Rwp'yl, Myx'yl, Gbr'yl,* and *Sr'yl* (= Istrael).

There were no details about individual feats of the giants in the Book of Enoch. Mani filled the gap with the help of the above-mentioned *Liber de Ogia nomine gigante.* This *Ogias* has been identified with *Og of Bashan,*[15] who according to late sources lived five thousand years and managed to survive the Deluge, thanks to his giant size.[16] But possibly stories that primarily appertained to *Ogias* were transferred to the better known *Og,* owing to the resemblance of their names. The name of *Ogias* is *'why'* (*'wḥy'*) = *Ohyǎ* (*Oḥyǎ*) in the Manichæan fragments, and this spelling is presumably more correct than that of *Ogias. Og* (*'wg*) indubitably would appear as *'wg* (or: *'wg*). Since Mani took *'why'* from an Aramaic text, the ending of *Ogias* cannot be regarded as a Greek addition.

12. Jackson, *Researches,* 37, 67 sq., has "poisonous mass"; See *OLZ.,* 1934, 752.

13. Hence the comparative *mzndr* (e.g. *Mir.Man.,* i) and the superlative Pahl. *mǎzan-tum* (e.g. *Dd.,* p. 118, 12 ed. Anklesaria).

14. Clearly to be derived from Av. *mazan-* "greatness." See also Jackson, *Researches,* on *mzn.* Hence, the first part of the name of *Māzandarān* probably = "gigantic."

15. Thus Dobschütz, *Decret. Gelas.,* p. 305.

16. Dobschütz, *Decret. Gelas.,* who quotes Fabricius, *Cod. pseudepigr.,* 799 sq., and Migne, *Dict. des apocr.,* ii, 649, 1295.

Ogias fought with a *draco,* and so did Ohya; his enemy was the Leviathan (text N). Ohya and his brother Ahya were the sons of *Šhmyz'd* (text H), i.e. *Στμιαζᾶς*, the chief of the Egrēgoroi in the Book of Enoch; hence, *Στμιαζᾶς* is transcription of *šhm-* (or *šḥm*?). In the Persian edition of the *Kawān* Ohya and Ahya are "translated" as *Sām* and *Narīmān,* but the original names are kept in one passage (A 60). The translator did well to choose Sām-Krsāsp, both with regard to Ogias' longevity (Sām is one of the "Immortals") and to his fight with the dragon (Sām is a famous dragon-killer). In the Sogdian fragments the name of Sām is spelt *S'hm* = *Sāhm,* as it is often in Pahlavi (*S'hm*[17] beside *S'm*); Ṭabari has *Shm,*[18] Sāhm's brother is *Pāt-Sāhm.* This name may have been invented by the Sogdian translator in order to keep the names of the brothers resembling each other. Narīmān was evidently not known in Sogdiana as a brother of Sām. According to the *Book of the Giants,* the main preoccupation of Sām-Sāhm was his quarrel with the giant *Māhawai,*[19] the son of *Virōgdād,* who was one of the twenty ers of the Egrēgoroi.

The *Book of the Giants* was published in not fewer than six or seven languages. From the original Syriac the Greek and Middle Persian versions were made. The Sogdian edition was probably derived from the Middle Persian, the Uygur from the Sogdian. There is no trace of a Parthian text.[20] The book may have existed in Coptic. The presence of names such as Sām and Narīmān in the Arabic version proves that

17. For example, *Men.Khr.,* 68, 12; 69, 12, ed. Andreas; *Pahl. Yasna,* 9, 10 (p. 71, 19).

18. *Shm,* of course, transcribes *S'hm,* not *S'm.* See Christensen, *Kayanides,* p. 130.

19. MPers. *m'hw'y* A 7, with suff. *m'hwy-c* A 19, Sogd. *m'h'wy* C 15 (= *Wrogdad oγlï* in B). Hardly = *Māhōi* (as suggested *ZDMG.*, 90, 4), for the ending *-ōi* was pronounced *-ōi* also in the third century (cf. e.g. *wyrwd* = *Wērōi* in the inscription of Shapur, line 34). Furthermore, there was no Māhōi among the heroes of the Iranian epos (M. is well known as the name of the governor of Marv at the time of the last Yezdegerd). More likely *Māhawai* was a non-Iranian name and figured already in the Aramaic edition of the *Kawān;* it may have been adapted to Persian. See *Mḥwy'l,* Genesis 4:18?

20. But see *Mir.Man.,* iii, 858 (b 134 sqq.).

it had been translated from the Middle Persian. To the few surviving fragments (texts A–G) I have added two excerpts, the more important of which (H) probably derives from a Syriac epitome of the book. Naturally, Manichæan authors quoted the book frequently, but there is only one direct citation by a non-Manichæan writer (text O). With the exception of text O, all the passages referring to the *Book of the Giants* (texts J–T) go back to Syriac writings (apparently). They are, therefore, to be treated as quotations from the Syriac edition. E.g. the Parthian text N is not the product of a Parthian writer who might have employed a Parthian version of the book, but was translated from a Syriac treatise whose author cited the Syriac text.

In their journey across Central Asia the stories of the *Book of the Giants* were influenced by local traditions. Thus, the translation of Ohya as Sām had in its train the introduction of myths appertaining to that Iranian hero; this explains the "immortality" of Sā(h)m according to text I. The country of Aryān-Vēžan = Airyana Vaējah,[21] in text G (26), is a similar innovation.[22] The "Kögmän mountains" in text B may reflect the "Mount Hermon." The progeny of the fallen angels was confined in thirty-six towns (text S). Owing to the introduction of the Mount Sumeru, this number was changed (in Sogdiana) to *thirty-two* (text G, 22): "the heaven of Indra . . . is situated between the four peaks (cf. G 21) of the Meru, and consists of *thirty-two* cities of devas" (Eitel, *Handb. Chinese Buddhism*, 148, on *Trayastriṃśat*).

21. The children of the Egrēgoroi share with the inhabitants of Airyana Vaējah, the distinction of being regarded as the inventors (or first users) of the arts and crafts.

22. For the spelling of *Aryān-Vēžan* see also Appendix, text U. It is not clear whether *Yima* (text V) had been given a place in the Sogdian *Kawān*. *Ymyẖ,* i.e. *Imi,* is the correct Sogdian form of the name.

TEXTS

This system (see below) of notation has been used also in my book, *Sogdica,* and in my paper *BSOS., X.* The various interpunction marks are uniformly represented by "oo" here.

(bcd)	=	damaged letters, or uncertain readings.
[bcd]	=	suggested restorations of missing letters.
. . .	=	visible, but illegible letters.
[. . .]	=	estimated number of missing letters.
[ ]	=	a lacuna of undetermined extent.
(84)]	=	same, at the beginning of a line.
[(85	=	same, at the end of a line.[23]

In the translation parentheses are employed for explanatory remarks.

FRAGMENTS OF THE KAWĀN

A. Middle-Persian

M 101, *a* to *n*, and M 911, fifteen fragments of a book, throughout small pieces from the centre of the pages. It has proved impossible, so far, to re-establish the original order of the pages. On purely technical grounds (size of the fragments, appearance of the margins, relative position of tears, stains, etc.), I at first assumed the following sequence: l-j-k-g-i-c-e-b-h-f-a-d-m-M 911-n. Being unable to estimate the cogency of these technical reasons now, because of the absence of any photographic material, I have decided to change the order of the first six fragments in the following way: c-j-l-k-g-i, in view of their contents.[24] Unfortunately we do not know in what order Mani had told the story of the giants. The task of finding the original order is made still more difficult by the fact that besides the *Kawān* the book contained one or two more treatises, namely: (1) Parables referring to

23. *BSOS.,* X, pp. 941 sqq.

24. But possibly *Frg. i* should occupy the first place; see below, notes on lines 95–111.

the Hearers, and possibly (2) a discourse on the Five Elements (here (1) = lines 160 to the end, and (2) = lines 112–159). The only fragments that undoubtedly belonged to the *Kawān* are c-j-l-k-g-i, while the position of the fragments e-b-h is particularly doubtful. It must be borne in mind that whole folios may be missing between apparently successive pages. In order to enable the reader to judge for himself, all the fragments (including the parables) are published here. The text is based on a copy I made nearly ten years ago (referred to in the notes as: Copy); a revision is not possible under the present circumstances.

Translation

(*Frg. c*) . . . hard . . . arrow . . . bow, he that . . . Sām said: "Blessed be . . . had [he ?] seen this, he would not have died." Then Shahmīzād said to Sām, his [son]: "All that Māhawai . . ., is spoilt (?).":Thereupon he said to . . . "We are . . . until (10) . . . and . . . (13) . . . that are in (?) the fiery hell (?) . . . As my father, Virōgdād, was . . ." Shahmīzād said: "It is true what he says. He says one of thousands.[25] For one of thousands. . . . ." Sām thereupon began . . . Māhawai, too, in many places . . . (20) until to that place he might escape (1) and . . .[26]

(*Frg. j*) . . . Virōgdād . . . Hōbābīš[27] robbed Ahr . . .[28] of -naxtag,[29] his wife. Thereupon the giants began to kill each other and [to abduct their wives]. The creatures, too, began to kill each other.[30] Sām . . . before the sun, one hand in the air, the other (30) . . . whatever he obtained, to his brother

25. = far less than he could say. Cf. *əž hazār yak, ŠGV.*, xiv, 2, *əž hazāra‿baewara‿yak*, ibid., xvi; Salemann, *Zap. Imp. Ak. Nauk, sér. viii, t. vi, No.* 6, 25, quoted Persian *az hazār yakī va az bisyār andakī.*

26. The texts *B* and *C* (Uygur and Sogdian) could be inserted here (or hereabouts).

27. Probably one of the twenty "decarchs" (Enoch 6, 7), viz. No. 4 *Kokabiel* = *Χωχαριήλ* in the Greek fragments, and *Χωβαβιήλ* apud Syncellus.

28. This also could be a "decarch," *Arakib- Ἀραχιήλ*, or *Aramiel- Ῥαμιήλ*.

29. Incomplete name.

30. Cf. Enoch 7, 5.

. . . . imprisoned . . . (34) . . . over Taxtag.[31] To the angels . . . from heaven. Taxtag to . . . Taxtag threw (*or*: was thrown) into the water. Finally (?) . . . in his sleep Taxtag saw three signs, [one portending . . .], one woe and flight, and one . . . annihilation. Narīmān saw a gar[den full of] (40) trees in rows. Two hundred . . . came out, the trees. . . .[32]

(*Frg. l*) . . . Enoch,[33] the apostle, . . . [gave] a message to [the demons and their] children: To you . . . not peace.[34] [The judgment on you is] that you shall be bound for the sins you have committed.[35] You shall see the destruction of your children.[36] ruling for a hundred and twenty[37] [years] . . . . (50) . . . wild ass, ibex . . . ram, goat (?),[38] gazelle, . . . oryx, of each two hundred, a pair[39] . . . the other wild beasts, birds, and animals and their

31. *txtg* might be appellative, = "a board." This would fit in three of the passages, but hardly in the fourth.

32. Evidently this is the dream that Enoch reads in the fragment M 625c (= Text D, below), which therefore probably belonged to the *Kawān*. It should be inserted here.

33. Here (or hereabouts) the texts E and F should be entered, both of which deal with the judgment on the fallen angels. Text F approximates to Enoch, ch. 10 (pronouncement of the judgment by God), while Text E is nearer to Enoch, ch. 13 (communication of the judgment the angels by Enoch).

34. = Enoch, 12, 4–5: *εἰπὲ τοῖς ἐγρηγόροις . . . . οὐκ ἔσται ὑμῖν εἰρήνη.*

35. = Enoch, 13, 1–2: *ὁ δὲ Ἐνώχ . . . εἶπεν . . . οὐκ ἔσται σοι εἰρήνη κρῖμα μέγα ἐξῆλθεν κατὰ σοῦ δῆσαί σε . . . περί . . . τῆς ἀδικίας καὶ τῆς ἁμαρτίας κτλ.*

36. = Enoch, 14, 6: *ἴδητε τὴν ἀπώλειαν τῶν υἱῶν ὑμῶν.*

37. = Syncellus, pp. 44–5 Fl.-R. (*ad cap.* xvi), cf. *Genesis*, vi, 3. *ἀπολοῦνται οἱ ἀγαπητοὶ ὑμῶν . . . . ὅτι πᾶσαι αἱ ἡμέραι τῆς ζωῆς αὐτῶν ἀπὸ τοῦ νῦν οὐ μὴ ἔσονται πλείω τῶν ἑκατὸν εἴκοσιν ἐτῶν.*

38. In Jewish Persian *trwš* is "ram" (Lagarde, *Pers. Stud.*, 73), but in the dialect of Rīšahr nr. Bushire (according to the notes made on this dialect by Andreas about seventy years ago) tîštär is "a young she-goat." See *JRAS.*, 1942, 248. [*trwš*, Is. 1[11], Ier. 51[40] = Hebr. ʿattūd, probably understood as "he-goat."]

39. These lines evidently refer to the promise of peace and plenty that concludes the divine judgment in Enoch, 10. Hence = "each pair of those animals shall have two hundred young"?

wine [shall be] six thousand jugs . . . irritation(?)[40] of water (?) . . . and their oil shall be[41] . . . (*Frg. k*) . . . father . . . nuptials (?) . . . until the completion of his . . . in fighting . . . (60) . . . and in the nest(?) Ohya and Ahya . . . he said to his brother: "get up and . . . we will take what our father has ordered us to. The pledge we have given . . . battle. And the giants . . . together . . . (67) [Not the] . . . of the lion, but the . . . on his . . . [Not the] . . . of the rainbow, but the bow . . . firm. Not the sharpness of the blade, [but] (70) the strength of the ox (?).[42] Not the . . . eagle, but his wings.[43] Not the . . . gold, but the brass that hammers[44] it. Not the proud [ruler], but the diadem on his [head. Not] the splendid cypress, but the . . . of the mountain . . .

(*Frg. g*) . . . Not he that engages in quarrels, but he that is true in his speech. Not the evil fruit(?), but the poison in it. (80) [Not they that] are placed (?)[45] in the skies but the God [of all] worlds. Not the ser-

40. *sārišn*: cf. *DkM.* 487*apu.*–488, 3, "when they provoke (*sārēn-*) him he does not get irritated (*sār-* and better, *sārih-*)." *GrBd.* 5, 8, "if you do not provoke, or instigate (*sārēn-*) a fight" (differently Nyberg, ii, 202). *sār-*, if from *sarəd-* (Skt. *śardh-*), is presumably the transitive to *syrydn* (from *srdhya-* according to Bartholomæ), cf. *NGGW.*, 1932, 215, n. 3.

41. Cf. Enoch, 10, 19: *ἡ ἄμπελος* [sic] *ἣν ἂν φυτεύσωσιν ποιήσουσιν πρόχους οἴνου χιλιάδας . . . . ἐλαίας . . . .*

42. *ty* or *ty*[*y*] = *tai* from *taih* from *taiγ* (cf. *GGA.*, 1935, 18), is ambiguous: (1) sharp instrument, (2) burning, glow, brightness, sunrays, etc. So also is *tyzyy:* (1) sharpness, (2) speed. One could also restore *ty*[*gr*].

43. Lit. "but the Wing(s) that (is, are) with him." The curious expression was chosen probably on account of the rhythm. For the same reason *byc* is employed in the place of *'n'y* in line 73.

44. Lit. "beats."

45. *'ystyh-* is obviously different from *'styh-* (on which see *BSOS.*, IX, 81), and possibly derived from *'yst-*, cf. *z'yh-* "to be born" from *z'y-* "to be born." *'ystyh-* is met with in *W.-L.*, ii, 558, p. 62 Ri 25, "blessed chief who stands (*'ystyhyd* ?) as the sign of the Light Gods." Lentz has *'ystyhnd,* but without having seen the manuscript one may presume a misreading (cf. ibid., R i 1, Lentz: *pd* [. . .] *dg*, but probably *pr*[*'d*]*ng*, R i 2, Lentz: *p.d'r*, but probably *pyr'r*, ibid., R ii 22, Lentz: *'n.z*, but probably *"wn*; for further cases see *OLZ.*, 1934, 10).

vant is proud, but [the lord] that is above him. Not one that is sent . . ., but the man that sent him.[46] Thereupon Narīmān . . . said . . . (86) . . . And (in) another place I saw those that were weeping for the ruin that had befallen them, and whose cries and laments rose up to heaven. (90) And also I saw another place [where there were] tyrants and rulers . . . in great number, who had lived[47] in sin and evil deeds, when[48] . . .

(*Frg. i*)[49]. . . many . . . were killed, four hundred thousand Righteous[50] . . . with fire, naphtha, and brimstone[51] . . . And the angels veiled[52]

---

46. St. John, 13, 18.

47. *phrystn: phryz-* = Parth. *prx'štn: prxyz-* (cf. Av. *pārihaēza-*, Sogd. *pr-γyž*; Parth. *'x'št*: MPers. *'xyst*) is mostly "to stand around, to be about, *versari,*" sometimes "to stand around for the purpose of looking after someone" = "serve, nurse, protect," often merely "to be." *phryz-* "to stand off, to abstain" is presumably different (*para-haēza-*).

48. The series of visions in which Enoch sees the arrangements for the punishment of the fallen angels, etc., and of "the kings and the Mighty" (chaps. xvii sqq.), follows immediately upon the announcement of the divine judgment. Hence, frgg. *k-g* must be placed after frg. l. Text G (below), which describes, the execution of the divine order, could perhaps be inserted here.

49. It is difficult to decide whether this fragment should be placed at the end or at the beginning of the book. The 400,000 Righteous may have perished when the Egrēgoroi descended to the earth. The "choosing of beautiful women," and so forth strongly suggests the misbehavior of the Egrēgoroi on their arrival upon the earth. The hard labour imposed on the Mesenians and other nations may be due to the insatiable needs of their giant progeny (Enoch, 7, 2 sqq.). On the other hand, "fire, naphtha, and brimstone" are only mentioned as the weapons with which the archangels overcame the Egrēgoroi, after a prolonged and heavy fight (Text G, 38), and the 400,000 Righteous may well have been the innocent non-combatant victims of this battle which may have had a demoralizing effect even upon the *electae.* To clear up the debris the archangels would naturally commandeer the men. We do not know whether Mani believed Enoch to have been moved out of sight (ἐλήμφθη Enoch, 12, 1) before the Egrēgoroi appeared, or before they were punished.

50. See texts R, and Q (where 4,000 instead of 400,000).

51. See *BSOS.,* X, 398.

52. See text T, line 3.

(*or:* covered, *or:* protected, *or:* moved out of sight) Enoch. *Electae et auditrices* (100) . . . and ravished them. They chose beautiful [women], and demanded . . . them in marriage.[53] Sordid . . . (103) . . . all . . . carried off . . . severally they were subjected to tasks and services. And they . . . from each city . . . and were, ordered to serve the . . . The Mesenians [were directed] to prepare, the Khūzians[54] to sweep [and] (110) water, the Persians to . . .

[On the Five Elements]

(*Frg. e*) (112) . . . slaying . . . righteous . . . good deeds . . . . elements. The crown, the diadem, [the garland, and] the garment (of Light). The seven demons. Like a blacksmith [who] binds (*or:* shuts, fastens) and loses (*or:* opens, detaches) . . . . who from the seeds of . . . . and serves the king . . . . (120) . . . offends . . . when weeping . . . with mercy . . . hand . . . (125) . . . the Pious gave . . . ? . . . presents. Some buried the idols. The Jews did good and evil. Some make their god half demon, half god . . . (130) killing . . . the seven demons . . . eye . . .

(*Frg. b*) . . . various colours that by . . . and bile. If. . . . from the five elements. As if (it were) a means not to die, they fill themselves with food and drink. Their (140) garment is . . . this corpse . . . and not firm . . . Its ground is not firm . . . Like . . . (146) . . . imprisoned [in this corpse], in bones, nerves,[55] [flesh], veins, and skin, and entered herself [= *Āz*] into it. Then he (= Man) cries out, over[56] (?) sun and moon, the Just

53. Cf. Enoc*h,* 7, 1 ?

54. On *myšn'yg'n* see *BSOS.,* X, 945, n. 2, on *hwjyg,* ibid., 944, n. 7.

55. *py*(*y*) always = nerves, sinews (not "fat" as in *Mir.Man.,* i, etc., as alternative rendering). It is equivalent to *nerfs* (Chavannes-Pelliot, *Traité Man.,* 32/3 [528/9]), Uygur *singir* (*T.M.,* iii, 18/9), Copt. = *Sehne* (*Keph.,* 96, etc.), Sogd. *pδδw'* (unpubl.). Cf. also *GrBd.,* 196, 4, where Goetze, *ZII.,* ii, 70, wrongly has "fat". MPers. *pai* = NPers. *pai* = Pashto *pala* = Sogd. *pδδw'* (not Av. *piϑwā-*).

56. Hardly "to". See Cumont, *Rech.,* i, 49, and my paper *NGGW.,* 1932, 224.

God's (150) two flames[57]. . . ? . . .,[58] over the elements, the trees and the animals. But God [Zrwān ?], in each epoch,[59] sends apostles: Šīt[īl, Zarathushtra,] Buddha, Christ, . . .

(*Frg. h*) . . . evil-intentioned . . . from where . . . he came. The Misguided recognize the five elements, [the five kinds of] trees, the five (kinds of) animals.

(160) . . . On the Hearers

. . . we receive . . . from Mani, the Lord, . . . the Five Commandments to . . . the Three Seals . . . (164) . . . living . . . profession . . . and wisdom . . . moon. Rest from the power (*or:* deceit) . . . own. And keep measured the mixture (?) . . . trees and wells, in two . . . (170) water, and fruit, milk, . . . he should not offend his brother. The wise [Hearer] who like unto juniper [leaves[60]. . .

(*Frg. f*) . . . much profit. Like a farmer . . . who sows seed . . in many[61] . . . The Hearer who . . . knowledge, is like unto a man that threw (the dish called)[62] *frōšag* (180) [into] milk(?). It became hard, not . . . The

57. Or: over the Just God, sun and moon, the (*or:* his) two flames. The "Just God" is the Messenger (not = *bgr'štygr,* i.e. Zrwān).

58. Unintelligible. Lit. ". . . two flames given into the (*or:* his) hand."

59. Cf. *Sb.P.A.W.,* 1934, 27, and *BSOS.,* VIII, 585.

60. Cf. M 171, 32 sqq. *'wṯ 'st ngwšg ky 'w 'b[w](r)[s] m'nh'g ky hmyw zrgwng 'štyd 'wš zmg 'wd t'b'n png ny ryzynd. 'w'gwn hwyc hwrw'n ngwšg pd pzd 'wd wšyd'x pd xw'r 'wṯ dyjw'r, kd dwr 'c wjydg'n 'wṯ kd nzd 'w wjydg'n, hw pd wxybyy frhyft 'wd w'wryft 'škbyd*, etc. "And some Hearers are like unto the juniper which is ever green, and whose leaves are shed neither in summer nor in winter. So also the pious Hearer, in times of persecution and of free exercise (lit. open-mindedness), in good and bad days, under the eyes of the Elect or out of their sight,—he is constant in his charity and faith." Although the word *'brws* is incomplete in both passages, its restoration is practically a certainty.

61. Possibly the parable of St. Mark, iv, 3 sqq.

62. *BSOS.,* IX, 86.

part that ruin . . . at first heavy. Like . . . first . . . is honoured . . . might shine . . . (188) six days. The Hearer who gives alms (to the Elect), is like unto a poor (190) man that presents his daughter to the king; he reaches (a position of) great honour.[63] In the body of the Elect the (food given to him as) alms is purified in the same manner as a . . . that by fire and wind . . . beautiful clothes on a clean body . . . turn . . .

(*Frg. a*) . . . witness . . . fruit . . . (200) . . . tree . . . like firewood . . . like a grain (?) . . . radiance. The Hearer in [the world ?], (and) the alms within the Church, are like unto a ship [on the sea[64]: the towing-line[65] (is) in the hand of [the tower] on shore, the sailor (210) is [on board the ship]. The sea is the world, the ship is [the . . ., the . . . is the ?al]ms, the tower is [the . . . ?], the towing-line (?) is the Wisdom. . . . . . . (214) . . . The Hearer . . . is like unto the branch (?) of a fruitless [tree] . . . fruitless . . . and the Hearers . . . fruit that . . . (220) pious deeds. [The Elect,] the Hearer, and Vahman, are like unto three brothers to whom

63. An elaborate version of this parable is found in M 221 R 9-23: *u nywšg ky h'n rw'ng'n 'w wjyydg'n ''wryyd, ''wn m'n'g c'wn 'škwh̲ myrd [ky] dwxt 'y nyq z'd hy, 'wd pd wryhryy 'wd 'gr'yyh̲ 'byr hwcyyhr hy. 'wd h'n myrd 'y 'škwh̲ 'w hwcyhryyh̲ 'y 'wy qnyycg xwyš dwxtr prg' myyh̲ cy 'byr h[wcyhr] [h]y. 'wd 'wy dwxtr 'y hwcyhr [ ]. 'wš 'w š'h̲ hndyym'n [qwnyh̲] 'wd š'h̲ 'wy qnycg ps[ndyh̲ ?] 'wd pd znyy nš'yy. 'wš [ ] pws 'cyyš z'ynd[ ] pwsryn 'yš 'c 'w[y myrd 'y 'š]kwh̲ dwxtr z['d* (remainder missing), "The Hearer that brings alms to the Elect, is like unto a poor man to whom a pretty daughter has been born, who is very beautiful with charm and loveliness. That poor man fosters the beauty of that girl, his daughter, for she is very beautiful. And that beautiful daughter, he presents her to the king. The king approves of her, and puts her into his harem. He has [several] sons by her. The sons that were born to that poor man's daughter . . . .". Throughout the story the *parabolic optative* is in use.

64. For a similar parable see below, lines 258 sqq.

65. *zyyg:* this word, hitherto unexplained, occurs in the *Šābuhragān* (M 470 V 14, spelt *z'yg*). The sinners, roasting in hell, see the Righteous enjoying the New Paradise, and ask them: . . . *'wm'n . . . z'yg 'w dst dyy[d 'wd ']c 'yn swcyšn bwzy[d]* ". . . put a rope (*or:* life-line) in our hands and rescue us from this conflagration." Cf. Pahl., Pers. *zīg*, Nyberg, *Mazd. Kal.*, 68.

some [possessions] were left by their father: a piece of land, . . ., seed. They became partners . . . they reap and . . . The Hearer . . . like . . .

(*Frg. d*) . . . an image (?) of the king, cast of gold . . . (230) . . . the king gave presents. The Hearer that copies a book, is like unto a sick man that gave his . . .[66] to a . . . man. The Hearer that gives [his] daughter to the church,[67] is like . . . pledge, who (= father ?) gave his son to . . . learn . . . to . . . father, pledge . . . (240) . . . Hearer. Again, the Hearer . . . is like . . . . stumble . . . is purified. To . . . the soul from the Church, is like unto the wife of the soldier (*or:* Roman) who . . . infantrist, one shoe . . . who, however, with a denarius . . . was. The wind tore out one . . . he was abashed[68]. . . from the ground . . . ground . . .

(*Frg. m*) . . . (250) . . . sent . . . The Hearer that makes one . . ., is like unto [a compassionate mother] who had seven sons . . . the enemy [killed] all . . . The Hearer that . . . piety . . . (258) . . . a well. One [on the shore of] the sea, one in the boat. (260) [He that is on] shore, tows(?) him that is [in the boat].[69] He that is in the boat. . . . sea. Upward to . . . like . . ? . . like a pearl . . . diadem . . .

(*Frg. M* 911) . . . Church. Like unto a man that . . . fruit and flowers . . . then they praise . . . fruitful tree . . . (270) . . . [Like unto a man] that bought a piece of land. [On that] piece of land [there was] a well, [and

66. Possibly "weapons."

67. Cf. *Kephalaia,* 192/3.

68. Cf. *āhīd-gar-ān* below, F 43/4. For a discussion of *āhīd* see Zaehner; *BSOS.*, IX, 315 sq. Perhaps one can understand Av. *āhiti-* as "something that causes shame", hence "stain", etc. In that case *Anāhitā* could be compared to *Apsaras.* As regards NPers. *χīre,* mentioned by Zaehner, this may be connected with Sogd. *γyr'k* "foolish." The word in *DkM.*, 205^{8}, is not necessarily *hyrg-gwn* (thus Zaehner, ibid., 312). It might be *hyl-* = Pashto *xəṛ* "ashen, grey, etc."

69. Cf. *supra,* lines 206–212.

in that well a bag] full of drachmas . . . the king was filled with wonder . . . share . . . pledge . . .

(*Frg. n*) . . . numerous . . . Hearer. At . . . like unto a garment . . . (280) like . . . to the master . . . like . . . and a blacksmith. The goldsmith . . . to honor, the blacksmith to . . . one to . . .

B. Uygur

LeCoq, *Türk. Man.,* iii, 23. Bang, *Muséon,* xliv, 13–17. Order of pages according to LeCoq (the phot. publ. by Bang seems to support LeCoq's opinion).

(*First page*) . . . fire was going to come out. And [I saw] that the sun was at the point of rising, and that [his ?] centre (*orḍu*) without increasing (? *aš̈ïlmatïn* ?) above was going to start rolling. Then came a voice from the air above. Calling me, it spoke thus: "Oh son of Virōgdād, your affairs are lamentable (?). More than this you shall [not] see. Do not die now prematurely, but turn quickly back from here." And again, besides this (voice), I heard the voice of Enoch, the apostle, from the south, without, however, seeing him at all. Speaking my name very lovingly, he called. And downward from . . . then

(*Second page*) . . . " . . for the closed[70] door of the sun will open, the sun's light and heat will descend and set your wings alight. You will burn and die," said he. Having heard these words, I beat my wings and quickly flew down from the air. I looked back: Dawn had . . . ., with the light of the sun it had come to rise over the Kögmän mountains. And again a voice came from above. Bringing the command of Enoch, the apostle, it said: "I call you, Virōgdād, . . . I know . . .

70. On *boγuq* see Bang, loc. cit., p. 15, who has: "the door of the closed (locked) sun." Acc. to *Enoch,* chaps. 72 sqq., there are 180 doors in the east one of which is opened each morning for the sun to pass through (the idea, familiar also from Pahlavi books, is of Babylonian origin).

his direction . . . you . . . you . . . Now quickly . . . people . . . also . . ."

C. Sogdian

M 648. Small scrap from the centre of a page. Order of pages uncertain.

(*First page*) . . . I shall see. Thereupon now S[āhm, the giant] was [very] angry, and laid hands on M[āhawai, the giant], with the intention: I shall . . . and kill [you]. Then . . . the other g[iants . . . (*Second page*) . . . do not be afraid, for . . . [Sā]hm, the giant, will want to [kill] you, but I shall not let him . . . I myself shall damage . . . Thereupon Māhawai, the g[iant], . . . was satisfied . . .

D. Middle-Persian

Published *Sb.P.A.W.,* 1934, p. 29.

. . . outside . . . and . . . left . . . . read the dream we have seen. Thereupon Enoch thus . . . . and the trees that came out, those are the Egrēgoroi (*'yr*), and the giants that came out of the women. And . . . . . over . . . pulled out . . . over . . .

E. Sogdian

T iii 282. Order of pages uncertain.

(*First page*) . . . [when] they saw the apostle, . . . before the apostle . . . those demons that were [timid], were very, very glad at seeing the apostle. All of them assembled before him. Also, of those that were tyrants and criminals, they were [worried] and much afraid.[71] Then . . .

(*Second page*) . . . not to . . . Thereupon those powerful demons spoke thus to the pious apostle[72]: If . . . . by us any (further) sin [will] not

71. Cf. *Enoch,* 13, 9, *ἦλθον πρὸς αὐτούς, καὶ πάντες συνηγμένοι ἐκάθηντο πενθοῦντες κτλ.*

72. Cf. *Enoch,* 13, 4–6.

[be committed ?], my lord, why ? . . . . you have . . . and weighty injunction[73]. . .

F. Middle-Persian

T ii D ii 164. Six fragmentary columns, from the middle of a page. Order of columns uncertain. Instead of A///B///CDEF, it might have been: BCDEFA, or even CDEF///A///B.[74]

(*Col. A*) . . . poverty . . . [those who] harassed[75] the happiness of the Righteous, on that account they shall fall into eternal ruin and distress, into that Fire, the mother of all conflagrations and the foundation of all ruined tyrants. And when these sinful misbegotten sons[76] of ruin in those crevices and . . . .

(*Col. B*) . . . you have not been better. In error you thought you would this false power eternally.[77] You . . . all this iniquity . . .

(*Col. C*) . . . you that call to us with the voice of falsehood. Neither did we reveal ourselves on *your* account, so that *you* could see us, nor thus . . . . ourselves through the praise and greatness that to us . . . -given to you . . ., but

73. i.e. the divine order for their punishment (*Enoch,* 10).

74. [Other fragments of the same manuscript ("T I"), not however belonging to the *Kawān,* show that there were three columns to a page; hence, the correct order of the columns is: BCDEFA. Perhaps this text, too, is not a fragment of the *Kawān.*]

75. *murzīdan* is "persecute, harass," not "show pity" as hitherto translated (*S* 9; *Mir Man.,* ii; *W.-L.*, ii, 556, r 6).

76. *ghwd* (*Mir.Man.,* ii), *ghwdg'n* (*Mir.Man.,* i), *ghwyn-* (*ZII.*, ix, 183, 27): the derivation of these words from *vi* + *hū* by Schaeder, *Sb.P.A.W.,* 1935, 492, n. 3, is based on the translation I had given; this translation, however, was based on nothing but this selfsame etymology.

77. 75. Enoch, 10, 10.

(*Col. D*) . . . sinners . . . . . is visible, where out of this fire your soul will be prepared (for the transfer) to eternal ruin (?). And as for you, sinful misbegotten sons of the Wrathful Self,[78] confounders of the true words of that Holy One, disturbers of the actions of Good Deed, aggressors upon Piety, . . . -ers of the Living. . . ., who their . . .

(*Col. E*) . . . and on brilliant wings they shall fly and soar further outside and above that Fire, and shall gaze into its depth and height. And those Righteous that will stand around it, outside and above, they themselves shall have power over that Great Fire, and over everything in it. . . . . . blaze . . . . souls that . . .

(*Col. F*) . . . they are purer and stronger [than the] Great Fire of Ruin that sets the worlds ablaze. They shall stand around it, outside and above, and splendour shall shine over them. Further outside and above it they shall fly[79] (?) after those souls that may try to escape from the Fire. And that . . . .

G. Sogdian

T ii. Two folios (one only publ. here; the other contains a *wyδβ'γ cn pš'qṯ δywtyy* "Discourse on the Nephīlīm-demons"). Head-lines: *R: pš'n prβ'r*[80] ". . . pronouncement", *V: iv fryštyt δn CC* "The four angels with the two hundred [demons] . . ." .

78. This passage in particular seems to show that the text is a fragment of the *Kawān.* There are two groups of sinners here: one is (apparently) to be transferred from a preliminary fire-prison to the permanent hell at the end of the world (= the Egrēgoroi), the other consists of the *κίβδηλοι* (= Giants). The digression on their final fate in the great conflagration, under the eyes of the self-satisfied Righteous (cf. *Šābuhragān, M* 470 *V*), is well in keeping with Mani's discursive style.

79. *w'y-* (different from Parth. *w'y-* "to lead") = "to fly" or "to hunt" ? Cf. *w'ywg* "hunter" (*BBB.*, where the translation should be changed), *Air. Wb.* 1356, 1407.

80. My pupil I. Gershevitch thinks *prβ'r* should be derived from *prβyr-*. It is true that "explanation, announcement" fits most passages better than "chariot"! Hence, Mahāyāna rendered as "the great announcement"?

✧ ✧

. . . they took and imprisoned all the helpers that were in the heavens. And the angels themselves descended from the heaven to the earth. And (when) the two hundred demons saw those angels, they were much afraid and worried. They assumed the shape of men[81] and hid themselves. Thereupon the angels forcibly removed the men[82] from the demons, (10) laid them aside, and put watchers over them . . . . the giants . . . . were sons . . . with each other in bodily union . . . . with each other self- . . . . and the . . . . that had been born to them, they forcibly removed them[83] from the demons. And they led one half of them (20) eastward, and the other half westward, on the skirts of four huge mountains, toward the foot of the Sumeru mountain, into thirty-two towns which the Living Spirit had prepared for them in the beginning.[84] And one calls (that place) Aryān-waižan. And those men are (*or:* were) . . . . in the first arts and crafts.[85] (30) . . . . they made . . . the angels . . . and to the demons . . . they went to fight. And those two hundred demons fought a hard battle with the [four angels], until [the angels used] fire, naphtha, and brimstone[86]. . . .

---

81. Enoch, 17,1: *ὅταν θέλωσιν φαίνονται ὡσεὶ ἄνθρωποι. pts'δ*, cf. Skt. *praticchanda-*.

82. viz. the human associates of the demons, esp. the "daughters of men."

83. viz. the giants and their children ? Or merely the children of the giants ? See below, *S.* to Syncellus (*apud Fl.-R.*, p. 25) there were three generations: (1) the giants, (2) the Nephīlīm, their sons, and (3) the Eliud, their grandsons. In the *Book of Enoch* the giants are killed, or rather incited to kill each other, before the Egrēgoroi are punished (ch. 10). Their spirits shall roam the world, until the day of judgement, as *πνεύματα πονηρά* (15,8–16,1).

84. This passage shows that the Sogdian text had been translated from either Middle-Persian or Parthian (MPers. *ky myhryzd 'c nwx 'wyš'n r'y wyn'rd bwd,* Parthian *ky w'd jywndg 'c nwx hwyn wsn'd wyr'št bwd*

85. *'nδyk* probably = skill, art, ability (differently, *BBB.*, p. 105).

86. See above, A 97. www.sacred-texts.com/chr/giants/giants.htm#page-69-note-8.

EXCERPTS

H. Sogdian

T ii S 20. Sogdian script.[87] Two folios. Contents similar to the "Kephalaia". Only about a quarter (I R i-17) publ. here. The following chapter has as headline: *"γšt š'nš'y cnn 'β[c'n]pδ[yh w]prs* = Here begins: Šanšai's[88] question the world. Init. *rty tym ZK š'nš'[y] [cnn] m'rm'ny rwγšny pr'yš[t'kw w'nkw ']prs' 'yn'k 'βc'npδ ZY kw ZKh mrtγmyt* (*'skw'nt*) oo *ckn'c pyδ'r "zy mrch 'zγyr'nt* = And again Šanšai asked the Light Apostle: this world where mankind lives, why does one call it birth-death (*saṃsāra*, Chin. *shêng-szŭ*).

. . . and what they had seen in the heavens among the gods, and also what they had seen in hell, their native land, and furthermore what they had seen on earth,—all that they began to teach (*hendiadys*) to the men.[89] To Šahmīzād two(?) sons were borne by . . . . One of them he named "Ohya"; in Sogdian he is called "Sāhm, the giant." And again a second son [was born] to him. He named him "Ahya"; its Sogdian (equivalent) is "Pāt-Sāhm." As for the remaining giants, they were born to the other demons and Yakṣas. (*Colophon*) Completed: (the chapter on) "The Coming of the two hundred Demons."

I. Sogdian

M 500 n. Small fragment . . . manliness, in powerful tyranny, he (*or:* you?) shall not die. The giant Sāhm and his brother will live eternally. For in the whole world in power and strength, and in . . . . [they have no equal].

---

87. Fairly cursive, difficult to read.

88. Probably by assimilation from *Šamšai* (= *Šimšai* in *Ezra*).

89. See above, G 28-9, and below, text M. According to *Enoch*, ch. 8, the fallen angels imparted to mankind unholy arts and undesirable knowledge, e.g. astrology, cosmetics, soothsaying, metallurgy, production of weapons, even the art of writing (ch. 69, 9).

QUOTATIONS AND ALLUSIONS

J. Middle-Persian

T ii D ii 120, V ii 1–5: and in the coming of the two hundred demons there are two paths: the hurting speech, and the hard labour; these (belong, *or:* lead) to hell.

K. Sogdian

M 363. (*First page*) . . . before . . . they were. And all the . . .[90] fulfilled their tasks lawfully. Now, they became excited and irritated for the following reason: namely, the two hundred demons came down to the sphere from the high heaven, and the . . . .

(*Second page*) . . . in the world they became excited and irritated. For their life-lines and the connections of their Pneumatic Veins[91] are joined to sphere. (*Colophon*) Completed: the exposition of the three worlds. (*Head-line*) Here begins: the coming of Jesus and [his bringing] the religion to Adam and Šitil. . . . you should care and . . .

L. Coptic

Kephalaia, 171^{16-19}: Earthquake and malice happened in the watchpost of the Great King of Honour, namely the Egrēgoroi who arose at the time when they were . . . . and there descended those who were sent to confound them.

M. Coptic

Kephalaia, 92^{24-31}: Now attend and behold how the Great King of Honour who is *ἔννοια*, is in the third heaven. He is . . . with the wrath . . . and a rebellion . . ., when malice and wrath arose in his camp, namely the Egrēgoroi of Heaven who in his watch-district (rebelled and) descended to the earth. They did all deeds of malice. They revealed the

90. Cf. *JRAS.* 1942, 232 n. 6.

91. 89. Cf. *JRAS.* 1942, 232 n. 6.

arts in the world, and the mysteries of heaven to the men. Rebellion and ruin came about on the earth . . .

N. Parthian

M 35, lines 21–36. Fragment of a treatise entitled *'rdhng wyfr's* = Commentary on (Mani's opus) *Ārdahang.*[92]

And the story about the Great Fire: like unto (the way in which) the Fire, with powerful wrath, swallows this world and enjoys it; like unto (the way in which) this fire that is in the body, swallows the exterior fire that is (*lit.* comes) in fruit and food, and enjoys it. Again, like unto (the story in which) two brothers who found a treasure, and a pursuer lacerated each other, and they died; like unto (the fight in which) Ohya, Lewyātīn (= Leviathan), and Raphael lacerated each other, and they vanished; like unto (the story in which) a lion cub, a calf in a wood (*or:* on a meadow), and a fox lacerated each other, [and they vanished, *or:* died]. Thus [the Great Fire swallows, etc.] both of the fires. . . .[93]

M 740. Another copy of this text.

---

92. If Mani's famous *Ertenk* was indeed a picture-book, this *Vifrās* may well have been the explanatory text published together with it; cf. Polotsky's suggestion, *Man. Hom.,* 18, n. 1, on Mani's *εἰκών* (but see *BBB.*, pp. 9 sq.). There is no reason for "identifying" the *Ertenk* with Mani's *Evangelion* (Schaeder, *Gnomon,* 9, 347). The fragments of the *Vifrās* (M 35, M 186, M 205, M 258, M 740, T ii K, T iii D 278) will be published at some other opportunity.

93. The point is that A eats or kills B, after B had finished C. A man killed his brother over the treasure, but was killed by a third party, etc. The Great Fire will devour the bodily fire which had swallowed the "exterior fire." Hence, Ohya killed Leviathan, but was killed by Raphael.

O. Arabic, from Middle-Persian ?[94]

Al-Ghaḍanfar (Abū Isḥāq Ibr. b. Muḥ. al-Tibrīzī, middle of thirteenth century), in Sachau's edition of Beruni's *Āthār al-bāqiyah*, Intr., p. xiv: The *Book of the Giants,* by Mani of Babylon, is filled with stories about these (antediluvian) giants, amongst whom Sām and Narīmān.

P. Coptic

Keph. 93$^{23-28}$: On account of the malice and rebellion that had arisen in the watch-post of the Great King of Honour, namely the Egrēgoroi who from the heavens had descended to the earth,—on their account the four angels received their orders: they bound the Egrēgoroi with eternal fetters in the prison of the Dark(?), their sons were destroyed upon the earth.

Q. Coptic

Manich. Psalm-book, ed. Allberry, 142$^{7-9}$: The Righteous who were burnt in the fire, they endured. This multitude that were wiped out, four thousand . . . . Enoch also, the Sage, the transgressors being . . .

R. Coptic

Man. Homil., ed. Polotsky, 68$^{18-19}$: . . . evil. 400,000 Righteous . . . . the years of Enoch . . .

S. Coptic

Keph., 117$^{1-9}$: Before the Egrēgoroi rebelled and descended from heaven, a prison had been built for them in the depth of the earth beneath the mountains. Before the sons of the giants were born who knew not Righteousness and Piety among themselves, thirty-six towns had been prepared and erected, so that the sons of the giants should live in them, they that come to beget . . . . who live a thousand years.

---

94. St. Wikander, *Vayu*, i [1941], 166, quotes my article on Enoch, and my paper in *ZDMG.,* 1936, p. 4, and remarks that *eigentuemlicherweise* I had forgotten Al-Ghaḍanfar's notice on Sām and Narīmān. Less careless readers will find Ghaḍanfar's notice quoted *in extenso* on the page cited by Wikander.

T. Parthian

291[a]. Order of pages unknown.

(*First page*) . . . mirror . . . image. . . . distributed. The men . . . and Enoch was veiled (= moved out of sight).[95] They took . . . Afterward, with donkey-goads . . . . slaves,[96] and waterless trees (?). Then . . . and imprisoned the demons. And of them . . . seven and twelve.

(*Second page*) . . . three thousand two hundred and eighty[97]. . . the beginning of King Vištāsp.[98]. . . . in the palace he flamed forth (*or:* in the brilliant palace). And at night . . ., then to the broken gate . . . men . . . physicians, merchants, farmers, . . . at sea. ? . . . armoured he came out . . .

APPENDIX

U. Parthian

T ii D 58. From the end (. . . *r š t*) of a hymn.

---

95. See above, A 98.

96. Cf. above. A 105 sqq.

97. Presumably the number of years supposed to have passed from the time of Enoch to the beginning of the reign of Vištāsp. The date for Enoch was probably calculated with the help of the Jewish world-era, or the mundane era of Alexandria (beginning 5493 B.C.), or by counting backward from the Deluge. Taking 3237 B.C. (but 3251 B.C. according to the Coptic chronology) as the date of the Deluge (see S. H. Taqizadeh, *BSOS.*, X, 122, under *c*), and adding 669 (= from Enoch's death to the Deluge according to the Hebrew Genesis), and subtracting the number in our fragment, 3,28[8 ?], from 3,237 + 669 = 3,906, the resulting date, 618 B.C., agrees perfectly with the traditional Zoroastrian date for the beginning of Vištāsp's reign (258 + 30 years before Alexander's conquest of Persia, 330 B.C.; cf. Taqizadeh, ibid., 127 sq.). From this one may infer that the famous date for Zoroaster: "258 years before Alexander" was known to Mani (Nyberg, *Rel. Alt. Iran,* 32 sqq., thinks it was invented toward the beginning of the fifth century).

98. The name is possibly to be restored in *Türk. Man.,* iii, p. 39, No. 22, R 5, where *wy.t'δlp* was read by LeCoq.

. . . gifts. A peaceful sovereign [was] King Vištāsp, [in Aryā]n-Waižan[99]; Wahman and Zarēl . . . . The sovereign's queen, Khudōs,[100] received the Faith,[101] the prince . . . They have secured (a place in) the (heavenly) hall, and quietude for ever and ever . . .

V. Sogdian

M 692. Small fragment. Order of pages uncertain.

(*First page*) . . . because . . . the House of the Gods, eternal joy, and good . . ? . .[102] For so it is said: at that time . . . Yima was . . . in the world. And at the time of the new moon (?) . . . . the blessed denizens of the world[103]. . . all assembled[104]. . . all . . .

(*Second page*) . . . they offered five garlands in homage.[105] And Yima accepted those garlands . . . And those . . . that . . . . and great kingship . . . was his. And on . . . them . . . . And acclamations[106]. . . And from that pious (?) . . . he placed the garlands on his head . . . the denizens of the world . . .

---

99. In quoting this text in *ZDMG.*, 90, p. 5, I took *wyjn* for what it seemed to be, viz. *Vēžan.* But as the appearance of *Bēžan* in connection with Vištāspa is incomprehensible, I have now restored [*'ry'*]*n-wyjn,* see above, G 26.

100. For the spelling, cf. *kwdws apud* Theodore bar Kōnay.

101. *'mwst* = *amwast* = believer, faithful (not "sad"!), from *hmwd-,* Arm. *havat-.*

102. Hardly "food" or "banquet"? Cf. Parth. *'wxrn,* etc. Also Budd. Sogd. *'wγr-* (*'wγ'r-*) Impf. *w'γr-*, Inf. *'wγ'wrt,* etc.) "to abandon" (*SCE.,* 562; *Dhuta,* 41; P2, 97, 219; P 7, 82; etc., appears to be of no use here.

103. Cf. NPers. *jehāniyān.*

104. Cf. *Vd.*, ii, 20 ? But the Manich. fragment appears to describe the election of Yima to the sovereignty over the world.

105. Cf. *BSOS.*, X, 102, n. 4.

106. *šyrn'm* is a *karmadhāraya,* = acclamation(s), cheering, cf. e.g. *Rustam frg.* (P 13, 5) *prw RBkw šyrn'm* "with loud cheers"; it should not be confused with the *bahuvrīhi šyrn'm'k* "well-reputed, famous" (e.g. Reichelt, ii, 68, 9; *šyrn'm'y,* ibid., 61, 2, cf. *BBB.,* 91, on *a* 11). But *šyrn'm* is also "(good) fame," see e.g. *V.J.,* 156, 168, 1139.

Fig. A.2. *Giant Warriors,* Bethoven M. Tiano (2016)

Notes

INTRODUCTION. ANTEDILUVIAN STRUCTURES

1. April Holloway, "Ancient Humans Bred with Completely Unknown Species," Ancient Origins, November 24, 2013, www.ancient-origins.net/news-evolution-human-origins/ancient-humans-bred-completely-unknown-species-001059?nopaging=1.
2. April Holloway, "Ancient Humans Bred with Completely Unknown Species," Ancient Origins, November 24, 2013, www.ancient-origins.net/news-evolution-human-origins/ancient-humans-bred-completely-unknown-species-001059?nopaging=1.
3. This and all biblical quotations not otherwise attributed are from the King James Version of the Bible.
4. Flavius Josephus, "The Works of Flavius Josephus," trans. William Whiston, Christian Classics Ethereal Library, accessed September 15, 2017, www.ccel.org/j/josephus/works/JOSEPHUS.HTM.
5. Flavius Josephus, "The Works of Flavius Josephus," trans. William Whiston, Christian Classics Ethereal Library, accessed September 15, 2017, www.ccel.org/j/josephus/works/JOSEPHUS.HTM.

CHAPTER 1. ANCIENT GIANTS OF IRELAND AND BRITAIN

1. "12′2″ Irish Giant," *Strand,* London, 1895, reproduced in Greater Ancestors, accessed September 15, 2017, http://greaterancestors.com/1194-2.

2. Chris Titley, "Thirsk—Enter a land of giants and curses and rediscover this North Yorkshire market town," *Yorkshire Life,* July 20, 2010, www.yorkshirelife.co.uk/out-about/places/thirsk_8211_enter_a_land_of_giants_and_curses_and_re_discover_this_north_yorkshire_market_town_1_1865946.
3. "7 foot skeleton near Stonehenge," *Historical, Topographical, and Descriptive View of the County of Northumberland,* 1825, reproduced in Greater Ancestors, accessed September 15, 2017, http://greaterancestors.com/7-foot-skeleton-near-stonehenge.
4. W. Max Muller and Kaufmann Kohler, "Amorites," *Jewish Encyclopedia,* accessed September 15, 2017, www.jewishencyclopedia.com/articles/1422-amorites.
5. "Anak," Abarim Publications, accessed September 15, 2017, http://www.abarim-publications.com/Meaning/Anak.html#.WgeqL7bMy_I.
6. "Giant Hand-Axe from Sheringham, Norfolk," *Nature* 135, June 8, 1935, 963–65, accessed September 15, 2017, www.nature.com/nature/journal/v135/n3423/abs/135963a0.html.
7. "Northumberland, England giants," reproduced in Greater Ancestors, accessed September 15, 2017, http://greaterancestors.com/northumberland-england-giants.
8. Walter Scott, "The Monthly Chronicle of North Country Lore and Legend," *Newcastle-On-Tyne,* 5, no. 1–5, 1891, 278.
9. "A Giants Skeleton," *Milwaukee Sentinel,* June 28, 1914, reproduced in Greater Ancestors, accessed September 15, 2017, http://greaterancestors.com/10-foot-high-skeleton.
10. "Dysarth Louth 3 10′ Giants," *Fielding Star,* XI, no. 2363, May 16, 1914, 4, reproduced in Greater Ancestors, accessed September 15, 2017, http://greaterancestors.com/dysarth-louth-3-10-giants.
11. "Island of Hibernia, Traces of Ancient Giants Unearthed in Ireland," *St. Petersburg Times,* 1951, reproduced in Greater Ancestors, accessed September 15, 2017, http://greaterancestors.com/island-of-hibernia.
12. John Milton, *History of Britain* (London: Ri Chiswell, 1695), 10–20.
13. Alan Ward, *The Myths of the Gods: Structures in Irish Mythology,* (*CreateSpace,* 2015), 15, https://www.scribd.com/doc/23476603/THE-MYTHS-OF-THE-GODS-Structures-in-Irish-Mythology.
14. Elizabeth A. Gray, trans., *The Second Battle of Mag Tuired,* Internet Sacred Text Archive, accessed November 11, 2017, http://www.sacred-texts.com/neu/cmt/cmteng.htm.

CHAPTER 2. ANCIENT GIANTS OF FRANCE AND SPAIN

1. Diodorus Siculus, *The Library of History,* Book V (Loeb Classical Library edition, 1939), chapters 28–31, accessed September 15, 2017, http://penelope.uchicago.edu/Thayer/E/Roman/Texts/Diodorus_Siculus/5B*.html).
2. "Montpellier France, Skulls 28-32," *Oelwein Register,* November 8, 1894, figure 40, reproduced in Greater Ancestors, accessed September 15, 2017, http://greaterancestors.com/montpellier-france-skulls-28-32.
3. Georges Vacher de Lapouge, "Le Gėant Fossile de Castelnau," *La Nature,* 888, 1891, 11–12.
4. Dr. Paul Louis André Kiener, "Le géant de Castelnau," *La Nature,* 992, 1892, 142.
5. M. R. Reese, "The Glozel Controversy: Amazing Historical Discovery or Elaborate Hoax?" Ancient Origins, December 24, 2014, www.ancient-origins.net/artifacts-other-artifacts/glozel-controversy-amazing-historical-discovery-or-elaborate-hoax-002493?nopaging=1.
6. "8′7″ Skeleton, Gap, France," *Evening Tribune,* November 16, 1935, reproduced in Greater Ancestors, accessed September 15, 2017, http://greaterancestors.com/8-7-skeleton-gap-france.
7. "Bones of Giant Are Unearthed near Paris," *Miami News,* December 26, 1918, accessed September 15, 2017, https://rephaim23.wordpress.com/2012/06/11/prehistoric-giants-of-france-and-spain.
8. "Skeletons of Giants Are Found near Paris," *Freeport Journal Standard,* April 15, 1933, reproduced in *Rephaim 23* (blog), accessed September 15, 2017, https://rephaim23.wordpress.com/2012/06/11/prehistoric-giants-of-france-and-spain.
9. "Skeletons of Giants Are Found near Paris," *Freeport Journal Standard,* April 15, 1933, reproduced in *Rephaim 23* (blog), accessed September 15, 2017, https://rephaim23.files.wordpress.com/2012/06/sevenfootneolithicgiantsfrancefreeport-journal-standard1933-04-15.jpg.
10. "Giants: Press Reports from the 19th and 20th Centuries," *Geraldton Guardian and Express,* April 1930, reproduced in *Frontiers of Anthropology* (blog), accessed September 15, 2017, http://frontiers-of-anthropology.blogspot.com/2014/04/more-on-french-giant-skeletons.html.
11. "Giants: Press Reports from the 19th and 20th Centuries," *Geraldton Guardian and Express,* April 1930, reproduced in *Frontiers of Anthropology*

(blog), accessed September 15, 2017, http://frontiers-of-anthropology.blogspot.com/2014/04/more-on-french-giant-skeletons.html.

12. W. A. Seaver, "Giants and Dwarfs," *Harper's New Monthly Magazine,* 39, 1869, 202–10.
13. Chris Chaplow, "Dolmens of Antequera," andalucia.com, accessed September 15, 2017, www.andalucia.com/antequera/dolmens-de-menga.htm.
14. Rachel Corbett, "A Journey Deep inside Spain's Temple of Cave Art," *BBC Travel,* November 19, 2014, www.bbc.com/travel/story/20141027-a-journey-deep-inside-spains-temple-of-cave-art.
15. "Update! Prehistoric Giants of France and Spain, Part 2.0," *Rephaim23* (blog), accessed September 15, 2017, https://rephaim23.wordpress.com/2014/02/17/update-prehistoric-giants-of-france-and-spain-part-2.
16. "Update! Prehistoric Giants of France and Spain, Part 2.0," *Rephaim23* (blog), accessed September 15, 2017, https://rephaim23.wordpress.com/2014/02/17/update-prehistoric-giants-of-france-and-spain-part-2.
17. "Update! Prehistoric Giants of France and Spain, Part 2.0," *Rephaim23* (blog), accessed September 15, 2017, https://rephaim23.wordpress.com/2014/02/17/update-prehistoric-giants-of-france-and-spain-part-2.
18. Brad Steiger, *Worlds before Our Own* (New York: G.P. Putnam's Sons, 1978) 51.
19. Nikolai F. Zhirov, *Atlantis: Atlantology: Basic Problems* (Honolulu: University Press of the Pacific, 2001), 215.
20. Ersjdamoo, "Giants of the Canary Islands," *Ersjdamoo's Blog,* September 26, 2012, https://ersjdamoo.wordpress.com/2012/09/26/giants-of-the-canary-islands.
21. Ersjdamoo, "Giants of the Canary Islands," *Ersjdamoo's Blog,* September 26, 2012, https://ersjdamoo.wordpress.com/2012/09/26/giants-of-the-canary-islands.
22. Ersjdamoo, "Giants of the Canary Islands," *Ersjdamoo's Blog,* September 26, 2012, https://ersjdamoo.wordpress.com/2012/09/26/giants-of-the-canary-islands.

CHAPTER 3. ANCIENT GIANTS OF ITALY AND GERMANY

1. Melissa, "Maximinus Thrax: The Giant Who Was a Roman Emperor Who Never Set Foot in Rome," July 25, 2015, www.todayifoundout.com/index

.php/2015/07/maximinus-thrax-7-foot-tall-roman-emperor-never-set-foot-capital-empire-ruled.

2. Chris L. Lesley, "Bones of an 8 Foot Tall Giant Lombardy, Italy," Greater Ancestors, December 7, 2011, http://greaterancestors.com/bones-of-8-foot-giant-lombardy.
3. Joseph Comstock, "Girgenti Sicily 10′6″," *A Tongue of Time: Girgenti Giant 1807,* reproduced in Greater Ancestors, accessed September 15, 2017, http://greaterancestors.com/girgenti-sicily-106.
4. "Giant Femurs Burma Grande," *Rephaim23* (blog), December 1, 2012, reproduced in Greater Ancestors, accessed September 15, 2017, http://greaterancestors.com/giant-femurs-burma-grande.
5. "Palermo Giant," *Easton Free Press,* July 31, 1909; *Euroa Advertiser,* September 22, 1893, reproduced in Greater Ancestors, accessed September 15, 2017, http://greaterancestors.com/palermo-giant.
6. Paola Harris, "Sardinia Giant Teeth," Greater Ancestors, November 11, 2012, http://greaterancestors.com/sardinia-giant-teeth.
7. "Ancient Race of Giant Humans Excavated in Munich, Germany," *Los Angeles Times,* May 6, 1934, reproduced in *Tnephilim* (blog), accessed November 11, 2017, https://encyclopediaancientgiantsnorthamerica.blogspot.com/2013/12.
8. Barbara DeLong, "Breitenwinner Cave," Barbara DeLong (website), 2016, accessed September 15, 2017, www.barbaradelong.com/special-projects/secrets-of-the-stones/the-breitenwinner-cave.
9. Chris L. Lesley, "Elongated Skull, Germany," Greater Ancestors, December 19, 2011, http://greaterancestors.com/elongated-skull-germany.
10. Chris L. Lesley, "Armor 8 Feet Tall," Greater Ancestors, March 17, 2014, http://greaterancestors.com/armor-8-feet-tall.

CHAPTER 4. ANCIENT GIANTS OF RUSSIA

1. John Jensen, "Super Megaliths in Gornaya Shoria, Southern Siberia," Academia, accessed September 15, 2017, www.academia.edu/6200990/Super_Megaliths_in_Gornaya_Shoria_Southern_Siberia.
2. Paul Seaburn, "Elongated Skull Found at Russian Stonehenge," Mysterious Universe, July 28, 2015, http://mysteriousuniverse.org/2015/07/elongated-skull-found-at-russian-stonehenge.

3. "Bronze Age Giants: Kurgan Warriors of Russia & Asia 7 Feet Tall," *Rephaim23* (blog), January 7, 2015, https://rephaim23.wordpress.com/2014/07/16/bronze-age-giants-kurgan-warriors-of-russia-and-asia-7-feet-tall.
4. "Bronze Age Giants: Kurgan Warriors of Russia & Asia 7 Feet Tall," *Rephaim23* (blog), January 7, 2015, https://rephaim23.wordpress.com/2014/07/16/bronze-age-giants-kurgan-warriors-of-russia-and-asia-7-feet-tall.
5. "Bronze Age Giants: Kurgan Warriors of Russia & Asia 7 Feet Tall," *Rephaim23* (blog), January 7, 2015, https://rephaim23.wordpress.com/2014/07/16/bronze-age-giants-kurgan-warriors-of-russia-and-asia-7-feet-tall.
6. "Bronze Age Giants: Kurgan Warriors of Russia & Asia 7 Feet Tall," *Rephaim23* (blog), January 7, 2015, https://rephaim23.wordpress.com/2014/07/16/bronze-age-giants-kurgan-warriors-of-russia-and-asia-7-feet-tall.
7. "Bronze Age Giants: Kurgan Warriors of Russia & Asia 7 Feet Tall," *Rephaim23* (blog), January 7, 2015, https://rephaim23.wordpress.com/2014/07/16/bronze-age-giants-kurgan-warriors-of-russia-and-asia-7-feet-tall.
8. "Bronze Age Giants: Kurgan Warriors of Russia & Asia 7 Feet Tall," *Rephaim23* (blog), January 7, 2015, https://rephaim23.wordpress.com/2014/07/16/bronze-age-giants-kurgan-warriors-of-russia-and-asia-7-feet-tall.
9. "Svyatogor," Epika, accessed September 15, 2017, http://epika.org/house-of-mythology/24-svyatogor.
10. "Giant's skeleton found by Soviets," *Washington Post,* October 30, 1945, reproduced in the *Nephilim Chronicles* (blog), accessed September 15, 2017 http://thenephilimchronicles.blogspot.com/2016/07/ancient-race-of-giant-humans-discovered.html.
11. "Laptey Sea Giant," *Lethbridge Herald,* February 6, 1946, reproduced in Greater Ancestors, accessed September 15, 2017 http://greaterancestors.com/laptey-sea-giant.
12. "Archaeologists Discover Strange Elongated Skull in Russia," Youtube, accessed September 15, 2017, www.youtube.com/watch?v=UMofrAm_xhE.
13. "Archaeologists Discover Strange Elongated Skull in Russia," Youtube, accessed September 15, 2017, www.youtube.com/watch?v=UMofrAm_xhE.
14. "Modern Armenian Fossils of Giants," Greater Ancestors, April 7, 2013, http://greaterancestors.com/modern-armenian-fossils-giants.
15. "Modern Armenian Fossils of Giants," Greater Ancestors, April 7, 2013, http://greaterancestors.com/modern-armenian-fossils-giants.
16. "Modern Armenian Fossils of Giants," Greater Ancestors, April 7, 2013, http://greaterancestors.com/modern-armenian-fossils-giants.

CHAPTER 5. ANCIENT GIANTS OF MALTA AND GREECE

1. Garry Shaw, "Malta: Island of Giants," *Timeless Travels,* reproduced in Ancient History et cetera, Febuary 11, 2016, http://etc.ancient.eu/travel/malta-islands-of-giants.
2. Lisa Zyga, "Researchers Demonstrate Acoustic Levitation of a Large Sphere," Phys.org, August 12, 2016, http://phys.org/news/2016-08-acoustic-levitation-large-sphere.html.
3. John Black, "The Hypogeum of Hal Saflieni and an Unknown Race with Elongated Skulls," Ancient Origins, January 2, 2014, www.ancient-origins.net/ancient-places-europe/hypogeum-hal-saflieni-and-unknown-race-elongated-skulls-001190.
4. John Black, "The Hypogeum of Hal Saflieni and an Unknown Race with Elongated Skulls," Ancient Origins, January 2, 2014, www.ancient-origins.net/ancient-places-europe/hypogeum-hal-saflieni-and-unknown-race-elongated-skulls-001190.
5. Philip Coppens, "Malta: The Small Island of Giants," Philip Coppens (website), accessed September 15, 2017, www.philipcoppens.com/malta.html (accessed September 15, 2017).
6. Philip Coppens, "Malta: The Small Island of Giants," Philip Coppens (website), accessed September 15, 2017, www.philipcoppens.com/malta.html.
7. Katie Allawala, "Adrienne Mayor on the Amazons," *Foreign Affairs,* June 15, 2015, www.foreignaffairs.com/audios/2015-06-05/adrienne-mayor-amazons.
8. John Noble Wilford, "Greek Myths: Not Necessarily Mythical," *New York Times,* July 4, 2000, www.nytimes.com/2000/07/04/science/greek-myths-not-necessarily-mythical.html?pagewanted=all&_r=0.
9. Hugh G. Evelyn-White, trans., "The Theogony of Hesiod,"1914, Internet Sacred Text Archive, accessed September 15, 2017, www.sacred-texts.com/cla/hesiod/theogony.htm.
10. "Gigantes," Theoi Project, accessed September 15, 2017, www.theoi.com/Gigante/Gigantes.html.
11. "Gigantes," Theoi Project, accessed September 15, 2017, www.theoi.com/Gigante/Gigantes.html.

CHAPTER 6. ISRAEL AND THE ANCIENT BIBLICAL GIANTS

1. "Numbers 13:28," Biblehub, accessed September 15, 2017, http://biblehub.com/numbers/13-28.htm.
2. Walid Shoebat, "Archeologists Discovered the Place Where Goliath Lived, Yet Ancient Goliaths Discovered in Israel Prove the Bible," Shoebat.com, August 17, 2015, http://shoebat.com/2015/08/17/archeologists-discovered-the-place-where-goliath-lived-ancient-bodies-discovered-in-israel-prove-that-there-were-several-goliaths-living-in-ancient-israel.
3. "1 Samuel 17:4," Biblehub, accessed September 15, 2017 http://biblehub.com/1_samuel/17-4.htm.
4. Adam Eliyahu Berkowitz, "Return of the Giants: Biblical Story of Goliath Proven True," *Breaking Israel News,* August 16, 2015, www.breakingisraelnews.com/46930/giant-discovery-israel-uncovers-proof-goliaths-rule-jerusalem/#t6Uyto1JL2lqVmTY.97.
5. Adam Eliyahu Berkowitz, "Return of the Giants: Biblical Story of Goliath Proven True," *Breaking Israel News,* August 16, 2015, www.breakingisraelnews.com/46930/giant-discovery-israel-uncovers-proof-goliaths-rule-jerusalem/#t6Uyto1JL2lqVmTY.97.
6. "Philistine Giants Destroyed," 2 Samuel 21:15–22, Bible Gateway, accessed September 15, 2017, www.biblegateway.com/passage/?search=2+Samuel+21%3A15-22&version=NKJV.
7. Adam Eliyahu Berkowitz, "No Fairy Tale: Will Giants Return to Usher in the Messianic Era?" *Breaking Israel News,* July 14, 2015, www.breakingisraelnews.com/45098/no-fairy-tale-giants-return-messianic-era-jewish-world/#DLFUtlwByV8djh0B.97.
8. "Numbers 13:32–33," Biblehub, accessed September 15, 2017, http://biblehub.com/numbers/13-32.htm.
9. Adam Eliyahu Berkowitz, "No Fairy Tale: Will Giants Return to Usher in the Messianic Era?" *Breaking Israel News,* July 14, 2015, www.breakingisraelnews.com/45098/no-fairy-tale-giants-return-messianic-era-jewish-world/#DLFUtlwByV8djh0B.97.

CHAPTER 7. ANCIENT GIANTS OF EGYPT, SYRIA, IRAQ, AND IRAN

1. "Bones of 10-Feet Men Found in Kalar Historical Sites," Aknews, July 18, 2012, reproduced in One Iraqi Dinar, accessed September 15, 2017, www.oneiraqidinar.com/bones-of-10-feet-men-found-in-kalar-historical-sites.
2. "Gilgamesh Tomb Believed Found," *BBC News,* April 29, 2003, http://news.bbc.co.uk/2/hi/science/nature/2982891.stm.
3. D. M. Mulhern, "A Probable Case of Gigantism in an Egyptian Skeleton at Giza," *Frontiers of Anthropology* (blog), December 2, 2013, http://frontiers-of-anthropology.blogspot.com/2013/12/a-probable-case-of-gigantism-in.html.
4. "A 38-Centimeter Long Finger Found in Egypt: Evidence of the Nephilim?" Ancient Code, May 21, 2015, www.ancient-code.com/a-38-centimeter-long-finger-found-in-egypt-evidence-of-the-nephilim.
5. "Dr. Ernst Muldashev," MojVideo, accessed September 15, 2017, www.mojvideo.com/uporabnik/rikisuave/slika/ernst-s-expedition-in-syria-looking-for-giants/296875.

CHAPTER 8. ANCIENT GIANTS OF AFRICA

1. "Giants Roamed the Earth Millions of Years Ago," MessagetoEagle.com, June 28, 2014, www.messagetoeagle.com/giants-roamed-the-earth-millions-of-years-ago.
2. Polly Jae Lee, *Giant: The Pictorial History of the Human Colossus* (South Brunswick: Barnes, 1970), 44.
3. Peter Kolosimo, *Timeless Earth* (New Hyde Park, N.Y.: University Books, 1968), 32.
4. Glenn D. Kittler, *Let's Travel in the Congo* (Chicago: The Children's Press, 1961), 30.
5. *The Travels of Marco Polo* (New York: Facts on File Publications, 1984), 175–76.
6. Alice Werner, "The Story of Liongo," *Myths and Legends of the Bantu* (London: George W. Harrap and Co., 1933), Internet Sacred Text Archive, accessed September 15, 2017, www.sacred-texts.com/afr/mlb/mlb12.htm.

CHAPTER 9. ANCIENT GIANTS OF AUSTRALIA, NEW ZEALAND, AND PACIFIC ISLANDS

1. "Timaru Herald from New Zealand 1875 reports of Giants Remains," *Timaru Herald,* February 24, 1875, reproduced in Greater Ancestors, accessed September 15, 2017, http://greaterancestors.com/timaru-herald-from-new-zealand-1875-reports-of-giants-remains.
2. "Timaru Herald from New Zealand 1875 reports of Giants Remains," *Timaru Herald,* February 24, 1875, reproduced in Greater Ancestors, accessed September 15, 2017, http://greaterancestors.com/timaru-herald-from-new-zealand-1875-reports-of-giants-remains.
3. Rex Gilroy, "And There Were Giants," *Psychic Australian,* October 1976, reproduction in Mysterious Australia, accessed September 15, 2017, www.mysteriousaustralia.com/strangephenomenonb.html.
4. Shino Konishi, "Inhabited by a Race of Formidable Giants," *Australian Humanities Review,* 2008, www.australianhumanitiesreview.org/archive/Issue-March-2008/konishi.html.
5. "Eight-Foot Chieftain," *Austin's Hawaiian Weekly,* October 7, 1899, reproduced in Greater Ancestors, accessed September 15, 2017, http://greaterancestors.com/eight-foot-chieftain.
6. Jonathan Gray, "Does a Giant Race Still Exist in the Solomon Islands?" Archaeology Answers, 2016, www.beforeus.com/giant_solomons.html.
7. William J. Thompson, "Te Pito Te Henua, or Easter Island," Washington, D.C., Smithsonian Institution, 1891, Internet Sacred Text Archive, accessed September 15, 2017 www.sacred-texts.com/pac/ei/ei14.htm.

CHAPTER 10. ANCIENT GIANTS OF EAST ASIA

1. Beth, "Pangu and the Chinese Creation Story," Ancient Origins, April 16, 2013, www.ancient-origins.net/human-origins-folklore/pangu-and-chinese-creation-myth-00347?nopaging=1.
2. "Giants in Asia," Biblioteca Pleyades, 2016, www.bibliotecapleyades.net/gigantes/Asia.html.

3. "Japan, 8-Foot Mummy," Greater Ancestors, 2011, http://greaterancestors.com/japan-8-foot-mummy.
4. Chris L. Lesley, "Huge Mummies in the Valley of the Giants," Greater Ancestors, 2014, http://greaterancestors.com/huge-mummies-giants.
5. Chiara Palazzo, "Dinosaur Footprint among Largest on Record Discovered in Mongolia's Gobi Desert," *Telegraph,* October 4, 2016, www.telegraph.co.uk/science/2016/10/04/worlds-largest-dinosaur-footprint-discovered-in-mongolias-gobi-d.
6. "Sam Poh Footprint Temple," Timeout, 2015, www.timeout.com/penang/attractions/sam-poh-footprint-temple.
7. Michael Newton, "'Cyclops Skulls' Baffle Tribal Folk," *Philippine Star,* February 24, 2012, www.bigfootencounters.com/hominids/cylcops.htm.
8. "Longest Sword Ever Excavated from an Ancient Japanese Tomb," MessagetoEagle.com, November 2, 2016, www.messagetoeagle.com/longest-sword-ever-excavated-from-ancient-underground-tomb-in-japan.
9. Brian Snoddy, "Giant Artifacts from the Tokyo National Museum," Genesis 6 Giants, 2016, www.genesis6giants.com/index.php?s=600.
10. "A Giant Footprint Has Been Discovered in China," Ancient Code, October 3, 2016, www.ancient-code.com/giant-footprint-discovered-china.

CHAPTER 11.
ANCIENT GIANTS OF INDIA

1. Mark Miller, "5000-Year-Old Skeletons of Harappan Civilization Excavated in India," Ancient Origins, April 18, 2015, www.ancient-origins.net/news-history-archaeology/5000-year-old-skeletons-harappan-civilization-excavated-india-002920.
2. "Giant Prehistoric Ape," *The Argus,* August 10, 1934, National Library of Australia, accessed September 15, 2017, http://trove.nla.gov.au/newspaper/article/10982620.
3. "The Mystical Giant Footprint and Ancient Pyramid in Lepakshi, India," Strange True News, January 24, 2015, www.strangetruenews.com/2015/01/the-mystical-giant-footprint-and.html.
4. Dhasa Maha Yodhayo, "The Legendary Ten Giants of King Dutugemunu," LankaNewspapers.com, January 15, 2011, www.lankanewspapers.com/news/2011/1/63722_space.html.

Index

Page numbers in *italics* indicate illustrations.

BOOKS OF RELATED INTEREST